Book List of Mary Goloversic

<u>Books for adults and teens:</u>

Three novels (published prior to 2019): Iron Heart, Living on the Edge, Raging Fire

True stories: I Married a Troll, Joys of Raising Boys, Woman in the Well, Death of a Mother

Self-help with God books: Diary of a Drunk, Games of a Gambler, Changing, God's Team, Scents for Women (Minutes for Men and Tips for Teens)

Success System books (godly success)—Successful Starts, Successful Love, Successful Forgiveness, Successful Communication, Successful Help, Success Club Manual, Success Memo, Travel to Success

<u>Books for children:</u>

Stubby the Stubborn Kitten (part of the Success System)

Stubby el Gatito Obstinato (condensed English/Spanish)

12 Critter Books—Water Gang, Capture Camera, Scamper the Shy Cat, Mischievous Mopsy, Candy the One-eared Cat, Bully Chase, Adventures of Boo Boy, Crandon the Curious Cat, Whiskers Watches, Walking the Dogs, Little Pets, Pet Parade

DEATH OF A MOTHER

MARY GOLOVERSIC

authorHOUSE®

AuthorHouse™
1663 Liberty Drive
Bloomington, IN 47403
www.authorhouse.com
Phone: 1 (800) 839-8640

Published by AuthorHouse 05/21/2020

ISBN: 978-1-7283-6174-1 (sc)

Print information available on the last page.

This book is printed on acid-free paper.

Scripture taken from The Holy Bible, King James Version. Public Domain

CONTENTS

ACKNOWLEDGMENTS

Thanks to the Gideons who provided the King James Version of the Bible by the National Bible Press in 1957

Thanks to my husband, Jim, for helping me with his computer skills and taking the back cover photo

Thanks to Pastor James Hill who officiated at my mom's funeral

Thanks to Tom and Ken Farley of the Bjork and Zhulkie Funeral Home in Ishpeming, Michigan

Thanks to the many people to helped me cope and recover

INTRODUCTION

We all had mothers who gave us life.
The death of a mother is hard at any age.
Death of a mother at birth is hard, because you never get
to meet your mother.
Death of a mother by birth, mother by adoption,
foster mother, or whoever helped to raise you
in childhood and teen years is hard,
because you miss mothering.
Death of a mother as an adult is hard,
because you remember all the years you had her.
Death of any loved one always leaves a hole in the heart
of the loved one left behind,
but we can go forward and live a full life.

This book is written in memory of my mother,
Myrtle Renowden Brandt

Each of us has had a mother and father, even if we do not know who they are/were. Even if a person's mother dies at birth, there can be a feeling of incompleteness.

Death comes in many ways to everyone, not only mothers—premature birth, illness, accidents, abuse, suicide, murder, drowning, bad habits (alcohol and other drugs, smoking, speeding while driving, etc.), wars, fires, floods, tornados—all sorts of ways, any age.

The author has lost loved ones from a granddaughter at the age of one day to an aunt at the age of 101. Some died of health problems, accidents, and "old age." The author, herself, has been close to dying many times. The word "death" is meaningful to the author.

The means of coping with the death of a mother that is covered in this book can be applied to the death of anyone. Even the loss of strangers can be hurtful.

Introduction to this Book

Think about these questions.

What experiences have you had with death?

Which of your loved ones have died?

How do you react to the deaths of strangers in the news from floods, fires, hurricanes, earthquakes, wars, alcohol/other drug-related deaths, car accidents, suicides, abuse, neglect, murders?

What lies about grief have you believed?

How have other people helped you to cope with death and grief?

Which Scriptures have helped you heal?

How can you comfort people who grieve?

Information in this book will help you answer these questions and other questions, too.

This book will help you recognize lies regarding death and grief and recover by finding and applying God's truths.

This book is a godly guide for grief, but, even if you do not believe the Bible, even is you are not a Christian, you can benefit from reading this book.

Although most of this book is about recovering from grief related to death, much of the information can be used for the pending death of a loved one and for preparing yourself for your own death.

This book will guide you to wade through the cesspool of death without drowning in despair.

A Note to You, the Reader, from the Author

I never planned to write this book about death, but, as I was writing <u>Woman in the Well</u>, a book about my battle with depression, my mom died. I added a section about her death in the chapter I had written about blame. As I was writing that chapter, it grew so long that I decided to write this book, <u>Death of a Mother</u>. It was hard on me spending four months writing these two books about death and depression.

We all have to deal with death. I wrote this book to help you, the reader. Some acquaintances have told me that writing this book will bring me comfort. The review of the Scriptures helped me, but bringing forth the sad memories was hurtful. Writing these chapters about my mom's death was hard, especially because the loss of my mom is so current in my mind—only a few weeks ago at the time I am typing this. Emotionally, this is the most difficult book I have ever written. I am writing these pages to serve God by sharing with you what I have learned.

I hope and pray that my sharing of this information will help ease the pain for some readers of this book who are mourning and help the readers of this book comfort others who mourn. "Blessed be God…Who comforteth us in all our tribulation, that we may be able to comfort them which are in any trouble, by the comfort wherewith we ourselves are comforted of God." (II Corinthians 1:3-4)

Also, the following pages have great examples of how to sort out lies in life situations, locate God's truths in the Bible, and apply these truths to our lives.

Lots of the lies I believed during my grief are presented in this book. This book includes extensive details, but they are important, because lots of the lies people tend to believe are presented and the process to replace lies with truths is presented.

Note:

Before I got this book to the publisher, I brought my old computer into a repair shop to have the documents from my old computer put on my new computer. However, the entire computer got lost.

It was a real set-back, but I didn't waste time worrying about it. I prayed about it and asked people to pray about the problem. I trusted God to answer the prayer in His time and His way. (My choice of time would have been instant, but it wasn't God's choice of time.)

I kept working on other books, kept going forward for God. A cheer in one of my children's books is: 'Go, go, go for God. Go, go, go for God. Go, go, go for God. Go. Go. Go." It's a good cheer for children and it's good for teens and adults, too.

Because of losing the computer, I am redoing the book—six years after the death of my mom. I've had to retype the entire book, plus I updated it for the six years that passed since the original book was written. Redoing this has been like living the grief over again.

You might notice that sometimes I used the past tense of verbs and the present tense of verbs within the same section of the book. Also, some parts are duplicated— some things are reiterated on purpose, such as some Scriptures, but some things that are repeated accidentally. In chapter 18, the notes are not in chronological order, because I zeroed in on meanings. Some things are accidentally not in chronological order. I have tried to avoid mistakes, but sometimes they accidentally happened as I put the pieces of these years of my life together like a jigsaw puzzle.

CHAPTER 1

THE DISCOVERY

Jim, my husband, was standing in the kitchen as I walked in the door from church around 1:00. He said we had to go right over to my mom's house. He said that something was wrong at my mom's house. He had gone up there around noon to plow snow and the blinds were still pulled down and the dog wasn't outside. He had peeked through a window and noticed that her bedroom door was shut.

We went over to mom's house immediately.

We looked in the old barn for the spare key she kept in the coffee can. It wasn't there.

I asked Jim to climb up on the porch railing and look over the curtains into her bedroom window. She was still in bed and that meant she hadn't fallen on the floor, unable to get up. She wasn't lying on the floor with a broken hip or stroke. I knew then that she was probably dead.

I remembered how, when she and I had returned to her house from an outing, she realized she'd forgotten to put her

1

house key in her purse. We'd gone to the police station, and an officer had come to her home and easily opened the door. I suggested to Jim that we go downtown to the police station. It was only a mile away. I thought the police could probably help us get in the house without breaking a door.

The officer at the desk told us that the police officers on duty were investigating a break-in at a bar, so two firemen came with us instead.

My mom's back door was bolted from the inside, so there was no simple way to get in. One fireman, with our permission, took one of his tools and smashed the glass in the upper part of the door, reached in, turned back the dead bolt, and opened the door. By then a police officer had arrived. We all went into the house, but the men told me not to enter the bedroom, to wait in the kitchen. The policeman said he had been in situations like that before, and he knew it would be better for me to stay in the kitchen. He stayed with me.

Thankfully, Jim took care of the situation in mom's bedroom and spared me that grief. Most of the men went into the bedroom with him. I don't know what the men were doing in the bedroom, but I heard one say that rigor mortis had begun to set in.

Minutes later the men came out with the news of the discovery that mom was dead. It seemed she had died in her sleep.

After the confirmation that mom was dead, I kept saying, "No. No. No." Over and over I denied the reality of her death, even though I knew it was real. I began to blame myself for her death.

Jim held me as I cried.

After a few minutes, I went into mom's bedroom. She was lying in her bed on her back, the covers nice and neat. Her eyes were shut and she looked at peace, just as if she were just asleep, except for a dribble of vomit on her face and what looked like a bruise on her chin.

I left the room and broke into sobs. Jim hugged me and held me tight.

I had noticed that mom had on mismatched pajamas. I sat the matching pajama bottoms nearby. Perhaps her water pill had worked and she didn't get to the bathroom in time and had to put on dry pajama bottoms.

(When I had to return to the house to pick up items for the funeral, I noticed that her partial plate and hearing aids were put away properly, so she must have felt well enough to have done her bedtime preparations as usual.)

I asked the men when they thought mom had died. One man said that from the amount of stiffness, he thought she had died several hours after midnight.

Knowing the rigor mortis had begun to set in, I assumed my mom had died in the peaceful position that she was in. I didn't have the courage to ask the men in which position she was when they found her.

There was little time for sorrow, though. Decisions had to be made.

Which funeral home should be notified? Jim and I conferred and told them the name of the funeral home.

We were asked if we wanted an autopsy. We decided against having an autopsy. The coroner was called, but didn't have to come to the house.

I knew that our oldest son who lived near us would want to see his grandmother before she left her house for the final time.

After I calmed a bit, I told Jim that I thought he should go and get Jim Jr. from work at the iron mine. Jim didn't think this was necessary, but I convinced him that Jim Jr. would want to see his grandmother one more time before she left her home permanently. Jim left to pick up our son.

While Jim was gone, the police officer stayed with me. I remember his gentleness and kindness. I don't remember the words, but I know the policeman comforted me with godly words of encouragement. I'm so thankful that God sent a Christian policeman to stay with me during the saddest time of my life.

When Jim and Jim Jr. arrived, Jimmy went into the bedroom to be with his grandmother.

I heard a vehicle in the driveway and knew the hearse had arrived. The funeral director, a young man, came in the front door. We had met him when we had attended other funerals. I knew he was a caring person, kind and considerate, and that helped. He spoke to us briefly, giving us his sympathy.

Then the time came to remove my mom. I stayed in the living room. The men went back to the bedroom and loaded mom on the gurney. I saw her wheeled out of the bedroom, her face covered. The gurney was steered to the front door and out the door. I didn't watch the loading of mom into the hearse.

Then the rest of us went to the kitchen and out to the back entry. At the back door, I stopped to pick up some of the broken glass. Jim said it could be done later, but I picked up the larger pieces of glass and the broken bits and put them in the trash. We went out, closing the door behind us.

It was Palm Sunday and the first day of spring. Mom had gone to bed on earth on Saturday night and woke up in her heavenly home to celebrate Palm Sunday with her Savior. (Even now as I type this, I am crying. It's been a few weeks since the funeral, but I have not adjusted to mom not being around. I know she is with God in heaven, but I miss her so much.) "For God so loved the world, that he gave his only begotten Son, that whosoever believeth in him should not perish, but have everlasting life." John 3:16

Phone calls had to be made. First we called our other two sons in the Army to tell them the news of their grandmother's death. They needed to get emergency leave.

Our youngest son, David, called back and said he had fourteen days leave and could come immediately.

Our middle son, Tim, and his family had just returned from picking up his adopted son in Thailand the week before (they had previously adopted a girl from Cambodia). All of them were tired. The boy was still in the period of adjusting to a new country, a different culture, language, and food, as well as a new family and a new home. It was decided that Tim would come alone and his wife and two children would stay home. Tim would be coming for only two days and then returning to his new son. We decided to have the funeral on Wednesday, the full day Tim would be with us.

I looked up phone numbers in the phone book and my address book and made many calls to inform people about mom. The calls were hard to make, but it was good to talk to the people, and the calls kept me from thinking in silence. Jim sent e-mails to notify many people in the United States and Europe.

It was a busy day, but, at time, I felt like David in the Bible as he wrote Psalm 55:1, 4-8.

"Give ear to my prayer, O God…
My heart is sore pained within me: and the terrors of death are fallen upon me.
Fearfulness and trembling are come upon me, and
horror hath overwhelmed me.
And I said, Oh that I had wings like a dove!
for then I would fly away, and be at rest.
Lo, then would I wander far off,
and remain in the wilderness. Selah.
I would hasten to my escape
from the windy storm and tempest."

CHAPTER 2

THE DECISIONS

The next day, Monday, the first sympathy card arrived from a friend. The entire day was a busy day, one of the most difficult days of my life.

One of the hardest things to do was going to the funeral home. I have no brothers or sisters, so there were only Jim and me. We didn't ask to look at mom.

We entered the office. We had to make many decisions. It seemed like an overwhelming flood of decisions, but at least my mind was kept busy on business. The funeral director was kind and patient, never pushy. That helped a lot.

DECISION We had to choose the pastor who would conduct the service; that was easy.

DECISION We had to decide if we wanted music and what kind of music—tapes or a soloist. I chose group-singing and an organist. The funeral director said it was unusual to have group-singing, but I knew the words of the songs would have godly messages that would benefit everyone.

DECISION We had to choose who would be pallbearers— our three sons and oldest grandson and a friend of our oldest son. (The friend's son was born with problems shortly before the funeral, so Jim Junior's friend could not be pallbearer, but a young man willingly took his place, though it must have been hard for him, because he had lost his mom in a car accident just a few years prior.)

DECISION We had to choose a prayer card with mom's information on it.

DECISION We had to choose a thank you card. I decided on prayer cards with woods pictures and thank you cards with a lighthouse. Mom liked the woods and lighthouses.

There were papers to sign.

I was asked to write the obituary and bring it to the funeral home.

I was asked to choose a dress and underclothing for my mom. I was told to bring her partial plate and eyeglasses. I was asked to find a photo for her hairstyle.

DECISION Then the three of us went to the basement to choose a casket. Caskets lined the walls and were stacked several high in the center of the room. Some were dark wood and some were light-colored wood. Some were metal—bronze, gray, and slate blue. Some had a woodsy picture inside the cover; some had an ocean picture. One was lined with a patchwork quilt. We chose a simple gray casket. I was glad when that decision was made and we could leave the funeral home.

(Thankfully a cemetery plot and a tombstone did not have to be chosen. Jim just gave mom's information to the monument person to add to dad's tombstone whenever the weather became warm.)

None of these decisions were extremely important decisions, but I realized why people need to pray and wait before making many decisions related to the death of a loved one—decisions such as choosing a casket, funeral arrangements, giving away things, selling things, using an inheritance. Some people make decisions before they die—buy a cemetery plot, make a will, give away special possessions, even plan the funeral. I knew one man who planned his funeral luncheon ahead of time and even chose to have his favorite chocolate chip cookies served at the luncheon. Advance decisions can lessen the burden of the survivors and prevent hurt feelings and quarrels.

DECISION We went to the flower shop to choose the flowers for the funeral. I noticed the pots of daffodils blooming in the store display window. Thankfully I knew the owner of the shop and one of the workers went to my church, so I wasn't among strangers. I knew I wanted spring flowers. I chose daffodils. My mom liked the color yellow. Also, Jim and I had bought daffodils for my dad's funeral. It was twenty-four years since my dad died, and it still bothered me to see a daffodil. I didn't want to add another kind of spring flower to the list of flowers that hurt me to see. I told the ladies I wanted a woodsy look. The owner suggested pussy willows. I agreed because my mom always looked for pussy willows to pick in the springtime, but I knew I wouldn't see pussy willows again without thinking about mom's funeral flowers. The lady also suggested a casket spray. I agreed and asked that it be made of daffodils to match the basket of potted live daffodils.

Another discouraging chore was done.

I talked to the pastor and he comforted me with empathy. His mother had died not long before. Our mothers were the same age and both of them had been born in May.

DECISION We discussed ideas for his message.

DECISION I chose four songs, two of which were my mom's favorites. I chose "I Have Decided to Follow Jesus," because it shows how we need to accept Jesus. The second and third songs were mom's favorites: "True-Hearted, Whole-Hearted" and "Bringing in the Sheaves." For the last song, I chose "I Know That My Redeemer Liveth" which I thought would be an encouraging way to end the service.

The time flew by. A lady from church advised me on the amounts of food to order for the funeral luncheon. DECISION Some of the funeral food was ordered from the deli of a local grocery store. The pastor volunteered to pick up the deli food. Several ladies from the church said they would bring food. Ladies from church volunteered to set up the tables, decorate, serve, and clean up afterwards.

DECISION I still had to write the obituary—to determine what to say in the article. Near the beginning of the article, I included the statement that mom went to sleep in her bed at home on earth on Saturday night and woke up in her heavenly home to celebrate Palm Sunday with her Savior. It was what had comforted me on the day of her death and would perhaps comfort others.

DECISION Jim took me to mom's house to choose which of her clothes would be best for the funeral. I was not in good condition to drive. It seemed very strange looking in her dresser drawers—I had never opened them before. I chose the underwear from the dresser drawers. I looked in her closets for a dress. There were several dresses, but a winter white outfit seemed to be the most suitable. She had bought it when she planned to marry an elderly man—years after my dad died, but neither of them wanted to leave their own homes in different cities, so the wedding never took place. I decided to add a lace insert of mine to the neckline. I found her glasses near her bed. It was difficult to look in her partial plate holder to be sure the teeth were in there. I was thankful to finish the task. We took a painting of my mother and dad to display at the funeral. Jim and I had had the portrait done from photos of them forty years before, when we lived in Spain, and we had sent it to my parents as a gift.

DECISION Choosing a photo for a hairstyle was difficult. Each photo brought me another memory of mom.

I went through many photos albums and bags of photos, but then chose a picture on Jim's computer that he had recently taken with his digital camera. It was a photo of mom and me at a book signing at our local library. That photo is on the back cover of this book; it's reminiscent of a happy day.

Jim dropped off the clothes, partial plate, glasses, photo, painting, and obituary at the funeral home. That saved me another sad trip to the funeral home.

I thought that a stuffed toy cat would look appropriate in the coffin with mom, because she liked cats. There are not many stores in our city. We checked at a department store, but the cats there looked like toys. I checked at a thrift store, but the cats there also looked like toys. Last of all, we checked at a Salvation Army thrift store and found a cat that looked almost like mom's Persian cat. It was perfect. The manager of the store had met my mom when we'd gone into the store many times. The lady was surprised that my mom had died, because we had been in the store only the week before and mom had looked healthy. The lady gave me the cat; it was her way of comforting me and it helped me a lot to know she cared.

People helped make Monday, the day after my mom died, easier for us.

My neighbor, who had been my friend for many years, came over to our house with a pan of goulash and she hugged me and listened to me and encouraged me.

In the evening, two of my friends came and visited and stayed quite awhile and were such a comfort to us. I was so glad they came.

"A friend loveth at all times..." (Proverbs 17:17)

Our youngest son drove home to Michigan from Virginia. It was wonderful seeing him, even though the situation was sad. He was a comfort to Jim and me.

It was good to have the goulash, because there was little time to cook.

CHAPTER 3

THE PREPARATIONS

On Tuesday, the day before the funeral, Jim and I went to the grocery store to shop for some of the food for the funeral. It was the same store I had brought my mom to shop for groceries for about the last twenty-five years. It was hard to go there to shop for funeral food. Thankfully, there wasn't much to buy—catsup, mustard, oleo, pop, coffee, tea, creamer, sugar, and napkins—so we didn't have to stay in the store very long. We dropped off the groceries at the church.

That same day, a friend from church brought over a pan of goulash. With our three sons, daughter-in-law, and grandson, the two pans of goulash from my two friends would go to good use. The friend stayed with me for half a day the day before the funeral. As mentioned before, I had no sisters or brothers, but she was a true friend, "…a friend that sticketh closer than a brother." (Proverbs 18:24)

I wanted a message of salvation for the people to read at the time of the visitation at the funeral home, so my friend from church took me to a Christian book and gift store to find a framed Scripture, but we couldn't find what I wanted. I did find a small white cardboard cross with fine sparkles on it. I bought it.

Then we went back to my house and I typed out the Scripture quote on computer in large bold font and printed it out.

"For God so loved the world, that he gave his only begotten Son, that whosoever believeth in him should not perish, but have everlasting life…"
John 3:16

Then she took me to several stores to find a frame for the Scripture and cross. We found an ornate gray metal frame that matched the coffin.

I put the Scripture and cross in the frame and then we brought it to the funeral home. My friend brought it in to the office to spare me having to enter the funeral home.

She kept pushing me to hurry. She knew our middle son would be arriving from Pennsylvania at the airport, and she knew I have a tendency to be late for appointments. It's a good thing she knew me so well, because, even with her pushing me, we were five minutes late picking up Tim, our middle son.

It was a comfort to have our three sons together with us for the first time in many years. (The two sons in the military lived far from us, so we didn't see them often.)

After we returned home, Jim and the boys went up into the attic of our home. Tim had brought a suit with him. Jimmy, David, and Jimmy III (our grandson) had no suits, so Jim brought them up to his suit closet in the attic to choose suits to wear. Then they went down to our bedroom and chose shirts and ties from Jim's closet. Thankfully, the four of them are close to the same size.

CHAPTER 4

THE FUNERAL

The next day was Wednesday, the day of the funeral.

After breakfast we dressed for the funeral. Jim Sr., Tim, David, and I got to the funeral home ahead of the hour set for visitation.

Everything was in place. The flowers were there—the flowers we chose, a container of two blue hydrangeas from Jim's family, an arrangement of cut spring flowers from my four cousins (my mom's three nieces and nephew), and a similar arrangement from my church family. The toy cat was with mom in the casket. The portrait of my parents was on an easel to the left of the casket. The framed Scripture was on a pedestal to the right of the casket.

It was hard to see mom in the casket, but it looked like she was just asleep. I kept reminding myself that mom was still alive and with her Heavenly Father in heaven.

Visitation began. The pastor and his wife were there. The church organist was there. Jim and I went up to the casket where we greeted the visitors.

One friend from church, the one who had befriended me the day before, arrived early and quietly sat at the back of the funeral home during the entire visitation and funeral. Just knowing that she was there was a help for me. Her presence was such a blessing.

Other friends began to arrive. One cousin came, the only member of my small family to come.

Jim Jr., his wife, and his son arrived. Jim Jr. broke down over and over.

The time for the funeral seemed to arrive sooner than we hoped. We went up to the casket to say our final good-byes before the lid was closed. It was so hard.

There were not many people there, so, instead of sitting in the room off to the side reserved for family, the funeral home director placed us in the front row in front of the podium. In some ways, that was better, because I knew the friends were nearby.

It was difficult to join in with the hymn singing, but the words of the hymns were encouraging and the music was uplifting.

The pastor read my mom's obituary and presented a beautiful message centered on the season of the year and the seasons of mom's life. He mentioned how he had talked to mom a few years ago and was sure mom had accepted Jesus as her Savior to assure her of eternal life in heaven. It was a wonderful message of hope, not a sad oration.

The funeral director then invited the people to the church for the funeral luncheon. The people were told they were also welcome to come to the cemetery for the graveside service of internment.

Then came the time for the removal of the casket to the hearse by the pallbearers. The family followed the casket out to the hearse. It was hard to watch the casket being loaded into the hearse. It must have been even harder for the pallbearers to do this final service for mom.

The police escorted the hearse and family cars to the cemetery.

The grave had been dug between my dad's grave and our granddaughter's grave. The large grave-digging machine was nearby. We had to wait for the gravediggers to get their tools out of the way. Two of the young adults there had loved ones buried nearby—the mom of one of the pallbearers and the baby of a young woman.

In a short time, the cemetery workers walked over to the grave-digging equipment to wait to finish their task.

Then the casket was unloaded onto a structure suspended over the open grave.

The pastor presented a brief message with prayer. It was a message full of hope.

Jim Jr. lingered near the grave to toss a bit of soil in his grandmother's grave. It was his baby girl who was buried between his grandmother and grandfather.

Then we all went to the church for the luncheon.

The tables were beautifully decorated. The pastor had picked up the prepared food from a grocery store—ham and rolls, potato salad, coleslaw, and a large sheet cake. In addition there was food donated by friends, including the church ladies. The ladies from the church had prepared a luncheon for fifty people, but there were few people there. The guests had waited for us to arrive to eat. Jim took photos with his digital camera.

The ladies of the church were in complete charge. I knew I need not be concerned about any of the kitchen work. The ladies worked quietly in the background, but I knew they were working with the love of God and the love of the mourners in their hearts.

At the funeral luncheon, I told the friend sitting at our table that my mom had been looking forward to taking walks as soon as the ice on her hilly driveway melted. The friend knew how much my mom liked to walk, because he had jacked up her porch a few summers before and gotten to know her well and had recently fixed her frozen pipes when we were out-of-town. He told me she'd be taking walks in heaven, not having to wait for the ice to melt so she wouldn't fall and break a hip.

It was then that I realized that, though I had planned to take mom to her favorite restaurant for chocolate pie the day after she died, in heaven, she wouldn't be disappointed because all the pieces of chocolate pie in the restaurant had been sold before she got to the restaurant (the last time we had gone for pie, the chocolate pie was gone and she had to settle for pumpkin pie), because there are no disappointments in heaven. I mentioned this to the same friend. The friend assured me that my mom was enjoying chocolate pie and walks in heaven. These words were a real encouragement to me, a reminder of how wonderful life in heaven is.

"A word fitly spoken is like apples of gold in pitchers of silver." (Proverbs 25:11)

After the funeral, we decided to go to camp to show Tim and David the changes we had made; we knew Tim would be flying out early the next morning. It was good to be at camp after the four stressful days.

In the evening, we went to a restaurant for pizza, a relaxing conclusion to a difficult day.

The next morning, Jim and I got up very early to get out middle son to the airport for his flight back to Pennsylvania.

Jim Jr. soon returned to working twelve hours a day, seven days a week.

David was still on military leave and his presence was a comfort to us. He suggested that the three of us take a trip to a city about a two-hour drive from our home. Here we visited a couple who were friends of Jim and David and me (he was a retired pastor—he and David had shared a lot of outdoor adventures together). These friends were an encouragement—they had empathy as well as sympathy, because the man's mom had died just a few years before and the woman's mom had passed years before. They understood and stood by me.

While there, we also visited a cousin. His mom had passed away within the year, so he gave his heartfelt condolences.

The travel helped to distract me from the thought of my mom being dead. It was an encouraging trip.

The rest of the days our youngest son was home passed quickly and enjoyably. All too soon, it was time for him to return to military duty in Virginia.

Our oldest grandson decided to stay with us for a few months and he helped to put my mind on the living instead of the dead.

CHAPTER 5

THE CONDOLENCES

Friends and family—even strangers—helped me survive the death of my mom. We received flowers for the funeral, food for the funeral luncheon, over 75 cards (many with heartfelt hand-written notes), lots of prayers, and a few phone calls. E-mail letters and e-mail cards arrived from all over the U. S. and several arrived from Europe. A relative in England lost his mom a week after I did, and we comforted each other; he had met my mom only a few months prior on a visit to the U. S. to find relatives!

People at church were kind to me.

The friends I mentioned previously were such a comfort to me the first three days after my mom's death. "Blessed are they that mourn: for they shall be comforted." (Matthew 5:4)

A new friend I had just made at church called often to check on me and uplift me (and she continued to do so for many weeks). She called at 10:00 every morning, the time she knew my mom had usually called me.

Friends called from Pennsylvania and Tennessee and Texas.

All these people demonstrated their friendship by being good listeners who patiently listened with sympathy and empathy, not criticism. They helped me to freely express my feelings and they encouraged me. They did what the Bible says to do. "Rejoice with them that do rejoice, and weep with them that weep." (Romans 12:15)

Of course, God was the greatest help of all. I talked to God about my troubles. "Humble yourselves therefore under the mighty hand of God…Casting all your care upon him; for he careth for you." (I Peter 5:6-7) "Cast thy burden upon the Lord, and he shall sustain thee…" (Psalm 55:22) "…God of all comfort; Who comforteth us in all our tribulation…." (II Corinthians 1:4) God will "…revive the spirit of the humble, and…revive the heart of the contrite ones." (Isaiah 57:15) I could then say as David said, "Therefore my heart is glad…." (Psalm 16:9) Some nights I prayed myself to sleep. As Jesus said, "Come unto me, all ye that labour and are heavy laden, and I will give you rest." (Matthew 11:28)

I listened to God's words of guidance and comfort and encouragement in the Bible, especially in Psalms. "Thy word have I hid in mine heart…" Psalm 119:11)

Even with the help of family, friends, and Scriptures, I went through terrible times of grieving.

Jim had put the photo disk on his computer and there was a continuous slide show of the photos of the coffin, flowers, and funeral luncheon on his computer monitor. I finally asked him to remove those specific pictures. He meant for them to be helpful, but, for me, they weren't.

The bills began to arrive from the funeral home and the flower shop. Utility bills arrived for my mom's house.

Sympathy cards continued to come, some with kind notes added to them.

I began to address thank you cards. I reread the verse on each sympathy card and the helpful handwritten personal messages. I reread the e-mails. I wrote a personal message on each thank you card.

I slept very little. I relaxed very little. I thought of mom when I went to bed, often woke up thinking about her during the night, thought of her when I woke up on the morning, and thought of her during the day. I remembered saying my final goodbye to her at her front door and I remembered seeing her in her coffin at the funeral home. I took prescribed medication to relieve some of the stress, so I could sleep at night, because I was exhausted.

I had many flashbacks of bad memories during the day. Over and over I relived the last three days she was alive and condemned myself for not doing more.

I also had many good memories of my childhood with my mom and even the last shopping trip and her last piece of pie at her favorite restaurant. Jim and I went to the restaurant once after she died, and the memories of being there with my mom crowded my mind to overflowing.

However, the bad memories and self-condemnation outnumbered the good memories.

CHAPTER 6

❖

THE DISPERSAL

The aftermath of the funeral was not easy, but people again made the process bearable.

The reading of the will took place the day after the funeral. I knew what it said prior, because I had given my mom a ride to the lawyer's office a few years before to make the will, but the contents of the will were a pleasant surprise for our sons and their children. The lawyer was kind and one of our sons knew his daughter and we compared news about the two of them, so that eased the sad situation. The lawyer told us to be sure to pick up mom's Social Security check when it came, so we could return it. Once, when Jim went to check the mail box, someone was lingering in the area; it was a dead end street. We had to be careful, so the check wouldn't be stolen, for we were responsible to have it returned. Death certificates were needed for the same procedures.

The thank you cards we purchased from the funeral home had a peaceful picture and kind words on them. Still, it took a lot of time to do them and I relived a lot of the funeral as I added the personal notes, but I wanted to show appreciation for all the people who helped ease our time of grief with prayers, cards, money, flowers, services, food, phone calls, and visits.

Jim went to my mom's house (now "my house,"—part of my inheritance according to her will) and replaced the broken glass in the entry door. He picked up her mail and paid the funeral bills. He cleared some leftover winter clutter around the outside of the house.

He plowed the snow for the rest of the winter weather and cut the grass in the warm weather as he had done for over twenty-six years since my dad got sick and died. He continued to pick up the mail. (The attorney advised us to keep the mail coming for six months to allow time for all the bills to arrive and be paid.) Jim paid the doctor bills, utility bills, and taxes out of mom's bank account. (It was a joint bank account and the names of both my mom and me were on the account and worded so either of us could use the account—I think the words "either/or" were used. Otherwise I would have had to wait to access the account and pay the bills. All of those bank details are helpful and should be done ahead of time—nobody knows the day of their death, so it is best to be prepared. Also, the will and other legalities are needed to prevent having to go though the probate procedure that can take a long time and end up in a lot of taxes to be paid.)

Jim's help in all of my mom's business and house affairs took a huge burden from me, but put the burden on his shoulders. His help let me avoid the stress of seeing her name on the incoming bills; to me, each envelope addressed to my mom reminded me that my mom was gone. It especially bothered me to go back to her house. I tried to go there with Jim several times, but it even bothered me to have Jim park the car in her driveway or even drive down the road to her house.

Jim had to take care of the empty house—turn down the heat on her water tank and furnace, disconnect her phone and cable, return her phone and cable box to the companies. At the time I wrote this, Jim had already done these chores and much more for over two months.

My friend from church—the one who spent a lot of time with me the week of the funeral—went over to my mom's house with Jim and packed up my mom's clothes to give to a mission. It was good to have a trusted friend relieve Jim and me of some of these chores. I wasn't there, but I think Jim probably did a lot at mom's house, too. I could not bear to go to mom's house, let alone empty out her dresser drawers and closets, the kitchen cupboards, the refrigerator, and all the other storage places. My friend organized everything well. She set aside mom's personal possessions for me to go through when the time was right. Not only did my friend complete those tasks, but she also went with Jim and me to deliver the clothing to the mission. That was better than Jim and I making the journey without her. Our conversation kept my mind off of my mom's clothes. Again she showed her loving Christian care. In addition to all else that she did, she cleaned my mom's house.

The people at the mission were grateful for the donation of mom's clothes. "As we have therefore opportunity, let us do good unto all men, especially unto them who are of the household of faith." (Galatians 6:10)

Someday I'm sure I'll want to look at the remainder of my mom's belongings and retrieve the cherished memories of her, but now is not the time for me to do those things. Perhaps that is why people are warned not to make rash decisions regarding possessions of a loved one who has died. (Even looking at gifts she had given me—a music box, a sweater she had knitted for me—bothered me.)

I had put a photo of my mom's house on the front cover of a novel I'd written, <u>Living on the Edge</u>, and I'd used her house and street as the setting for the story. Whenever I saw that book, I'd remember her and her house and our walks along the creek near her house (the creek is also in the cover photo).

For over twenty years, mom had attended the same church as me, and, on the first Sunday after the funeral, I saw the pew in the back of the church where she had sat with her gentleman friend all those years.

The funeral flowers presented a problem for me. They were so beautiful, that I wanted to share their beauty at church. The flowers were brought to church, but, on Sunday morning, all I could see when I looked at them was how they had looked beside my mom's coffin, especially the flowers that were going to be planted on my mom's and dad's graves. It was March and snow was still on the frozen ground, so planting season was months away. (Eventually the cut flowers wilted, and a lady at church offered me the basket and driftwood from the floral arrangement, but I told her to keep them. I like driftwood and baskets, but I didn't want any reminders of the funeral.)

Later that week, I dropped a note in the church mailbox (a group of cubbyholes to hold mail—each person who regularly attends church has a mail compartment there) to a lady who did a lot of the flower arranging at church. In the note, I asked her to find someone to take the plants home and take care of them until springtime, when the daffodils and hydrangeas could be planted at the graves. She took the plants to her own home. Many weeks later, when she went out-of-town, she gave them to another lady—the lady who had done so much for me, including the boxing of my mom's clothes, at the time of mom's death. (As I type this manuscript, this friend at church also said she planned to plant the plants at the cemetery for me soon. She knows how upsetting it is for me to go to the graves of loved ones. This friend is really sticking with me all the way through my time of grief.)

I made five visits to my mom's house after she died.

One visit was the day she died.

The second visit to the house was at the time of preparing for the funeral. As mentioned before, after my mom died, I had to go there to choose a dress for her funeral and find her partial plate and other items for the funeral.

The third visit to the house was the day after the funeral. Two cousins from Wisconsin (hundreds of miles away) came the day after the funeral. I wanted to give them something to remind them of my mom, so I forced myself to go over to my mom's home while they chose a few dishes. It was difficult, but still it was a blessing. (I would have been glad to give them many items, but my heartbroken oldest son was finding it hard to let go of anything of his grandmother's—nothing was valuable, but everything was meaningful to him.) It was difficult to go there, but still it was a blessing. One of these cousins had spent her teenage years in a neighboring town, so we had shared memories of mom as we grew up. The cousins shared one current memory that didn't bother me. We recalled the skunk that came to visit my mom the last time my cousins had visited her, just a few weeks before she died. The skunk had greeted us at mom's front door. This was the same door where I had said my last goodbyes to mom and it was the same door where my cousins said their last goodbyes to her,

BUT, with a skunk. It was a humorous memory. Sharing that memory helped ease my hurting heart a little. I don't have heart trouble, but I felt like I had a hole in my heart.

The fourth visit to my mom's house was with our oldest son who wants to buy my mom's home. He already had plans for some changes and was enthusiastic as he pointed out his plans to me. This was encouraging for me, because I pictured him in the rooms of the house instead of my mom. This son likes to go to the house and just touch the belongings of his grandparents. One of our sons wanted only a mantel clock from his grandmother's house. Another of our sons wanted nothing, though he had fond memories of visiting her there and taking her on many walks in the woods and on day trips. We all remember mom in different ways.

The fifth visit to my mom's house was to show it to a man from Oregon whose grandmother lived there decades ago. His grandfather was a mining captain at the same mine my grandfather captained. The man was jolly and had funny memories to relate. He had come all the way from Oregon, the first time to visit our city in about fifteen years. On his prior visit, he had seen my mom sitting on the porch, but, being a stranger in town, he didn't want to scare her by going up to the porch. This man's timing (actually it was probably God's timing) for asking to see the house was perfect, because it was easier for me to go up there with a stranger. Also, I was seeing the history of the house before mom lived there.

It was a relief to peek at the far past of the house with that man from Oregon, the near past of the house with my cousins, and the future of the house if my son buys the house, rather than dwell on the death of my mom in her house. However, to peek at the house in the present—the house vacated by mom—was still unbearable for me. Though I attempted to go to the house several times, and even got as far as the driveway once, I didn't go near the house for years after the last visit.

Soon the funeral chores were done, around the same time, most people stopped coming over and calling.

There was a big gap in each day after over twenty-six years (counting the two years of my dad's illness) of being busy helping mom do her errands, taking her on outings, and having long daily phone calls with her at ten o'clock every day (except Sunday or days I was called to work at school—those days the calls were later in the day) and also at other times of the day. It was a big change and it took me a long time to fill the gaps in the schedule with my friends and in other ways.

CHAPTER 7

THE RECALL

Even though I didn't go to my mom's house, I still kept reliving in my mind the last four days of her life.

I never seemed to be able to forget that last Friday I saw my mom alive. I will probably always regret my being in a hurry that day.

On the Tuesday of that week, Jim and I had cleared out mom's upstairs back bedroom for her. Previously she had piled up lots of clothes to give to a thrift shop, so Jim and I bagged the clothes—I told her to sit and just give us instructions about what to put in the bag. We also moved things around in the room. Then I cleared and organized the rest of the clutter. Jim loaded the heavy bags into my car to give away. Mom was really pleased with the neat look of her back bedroom.

Mom seemed to be in the spring-cleaning mood. (After her previous heart attack, the doctor said she had congestive heart failure, and he had ordered her never to do heavy cleaning again. I have degenerated vertebrae and disks in my back and can no longer do heavy cleaning, raking, or other heavy or bending chores. Mom refused to have a friend of mine come in and do her heavy cleaning.)

Mom said she had been moving insulation around in the basement. (We had recently gotten people to come in and weatherproof her house, because she said the house was cold even with the furnace running a lot. Apparently some insulation had been left behind. When she mentioned that, I had told her to wait for Jim or our son or grandson to sweep the basement, but she said she had already finished it.)

Mom also said she had been raking the winter supply of dog droppings, even though people were scheduled to come and do her raking when warm weather arrived. (Our oldest son had removed many of the dog droppings over the winter.) I reminded her that the garden workers would be coming to rake and that she was not supposed to rake. I knew she enjoyed being outside, but that she should not rake.

On Thursday mom called to say that her legs felt swollen. She said she probably just strained them reaching to plug in the vacuum or cleaning too much. I offered to take her to the doctor or emergency room at the hospital, but she wouldn't go.

The next day, Friday, she phoned and again said her legs felt swollen. I think she mentioned that she wondered if there was a circulation problem (or she may have said that the previous day). Immediately I drove over to her house to check her legs. They may have been a little larger than usual, but they didn't look swollen much, if at all. I could see her ankles.

However, I didn't have my reading glasses on. Also, I didn't know how her legs looked normally, because it was cold weather and I had only seen her bare legs once (at the doctor's office) since the previous summer. A few days before, I had seen a woman in a chiropractor's office with her legs swollen like elephant legs and she was still walking and talking and smiling, but the doctor had advised that lady to go to the hospital on her way home. I could still even see mom's anklebones. (I think I remembered the elephant-like legs I had seen recently; there were no ankles visible on those legs.) I saw a few of mom's veins protruding a bit, but I didn't think much of that, because I have varicose veins and I'm used to seeing large veins. I didn't repeat the offer of taking her for a medical checkup, because her legs seemed all right. She didn't ask to go for a checkup.

I looked at the outlet she usually used for her vacuum. I offered to ask Jim to move the bookcase for easier access to an outlet, but she said it wasn't necessary. She said she used a different outlet that she could easily reach. Her vacuum is self-propelled, so it is light to use.

I don't know why, but I was in a rush that Friday, possibly to finish typing my book about depression (<u>Woman in the Well</u>) before I left for retreat the next day or it might have been the day I planned to deliver mom's bags of discarded clothes to the thrift shop. I didn't take time to sit with mom or have a cup of tea, but went to the door to leave.

At the door I hesitantly told her I planned to go to a retreat the next day. (I didn't think to tell her it was only a day retreat, and I'd be back the same night. The fall retreat is three days, but the winter retreat is only six hours, plus two hours of travel time each way. I hadn't even planned to go to the winter retreat, but someone who hadn't ever gone to the retreat had asked me to go, so she'd have someone she knew with her.) I was thinking about canceling my plans to make sure mom was okay. She must have read my mind, because she unselfishly said, "You go to the retreat." Actually, I would have gladly skipped retreat to help my mom, but it didn't seem necessary, because she was walking well and didn't mention any chest pains or other nasty symptoms.

I said that we'd go to her favorite restaurant for her favorite dessert, chocolate pie, on Monday.

I'm sure she gave me a hug and I hugged her back. (I hadn't been much of a hugger since I was a little girl, but I was gradually improving on giving and receiving hugs.)

As a last-minute thought, I said to call 911 if she had any problem while I was gone. My son and his wife and Jim would be home off and on the next day, but I knew they had plans for part of the day, so I wanted to be sure mom could reach help if she needed it. I'd never told her to call 911 before. (I had tried to get her to have Lifeline installed many times before, but she refused.)

Saturday I went to the retreat as planned, but I got home from the retreat about three hours later than I expected to return (the people with whom I rode waited to get tapes of the retreat made and then stopped for dinner on the way home—I had only pop and a Rice Crispy bar). Jim and I had planned to attend a fundraiser dinner around 5:30 for a friend of ours who has cancer. I got home from the retreat at 8 PM.

I drove right to the fundraiser event. Jim was in the parking lot and said he had a carryout dinner in the truck for me. I went inside to talk to my friend for a few minutes, and then I stuck around a little while to see if I could be of help clearing up, but her family and volunteers had it all under control.

I returned home and ate part of my dinner. I was physically exhausted, but my mind was still in high gear from the euphoria of the retreat. I excitedly told Jim about the retreat. I forgot to call my mom. I didn't see my reminder note on our kitchen table until much later on the next day, Sunday, when I finally slowed down enough to look at the many papers on my cluttered kitchen table. The note said: "Check on mom."

She was alive during the very early hours on Sunday morning, but I was sound asleep, not suspecting that she was close to death.

Paul, in the Bible, committed terrible sins against Christians, but he was able to put the past behind him. He said, "...this one thing I do, forgetting those things which are behind, and reaching forth unto those things which are before...." (Philippians 3:13) Paul put his bad memories behind and moved forward for God.

I was stuck in the rut of recalling regrets. These memories kept replaying over and over in my mind, like spinning my wheels in mud and going nowhere.

I couldn't go back and relive that Friday, the last day I saw her alive. However, the memories of those last four days—Thursday through Sunday—kept replaying in my mind, over and over and over again for about two months. Rerun after rerun played in my mind.

My imagination goes to good use in my creative writing, but my imagination also made those memories vivid for me. I went to bed at night thinking those thoughts and woke up during the night thinking those thoughts and woke up in the morning thinking those thoughts. I'd keep thinking those thoughts off and on all day, every day. As I thought those thoughts about mom's last days on earth, I added thoughts of my self-blame for her death.

I visualized my mom saying "Goodbye" to me at her front door on Friday, dead in her coffin at the funeral home, dead in her grave between my dad and my granddaughter.

I even had trouble sleeping in the bed in our house where she had her first heart attack. (I use that room when Jim snores and our grandson is in the other spare bedroom.) Mom survived that heart attack, so that room should bring good memories, not bad ones.

My mom and grandmother used to say that my grandmother was sensitive, my mom was more sensitive, and Mary was the most sensitive of all.

My cat had died less than a year before my mom. Jim found a cat that looked almost like the cat that died; the new cat was full of mischief and fun that helped me overcome the loss of my cat.

When our dog died a year ago, Jim wanted to bury her at our camp. I said to bury her about five miles north of our camp, so I wouldn't think about her quite as often. For a week, I could picture coyotes digging her up and tearing her apart and all sorts of other things. I drove out, dug her up, checked her, brought her to camp, and had Jim rebury her on the back lot across the road from our camp. Now I haven't been able to walk the path that goes by the dog's grave, because I feel too sad.

One day when I took my mom grocery shopping, there was an ad on the bulletin board for puppies. We went to look at the puppies. My mom bought me a puppy that resembled my dog that had died. The puppy, like the cat, was full of mischief and full of fun and helped me overcome the loss of my dog. However, when my mom died, whenever I saw my puppy, I'd remember my mom and miss her.

I knew nobody could replace my mom.

Yes, I am very sensitive.

So many things jogged good memories of my mom, but even the good memories hurt me for several months, The good memories would remind me that she was dead, so even the good memories were hard for me to handle.

Even reminders of those who died decades ago sometimes make me sad. I have clumps of my grandmother's bleeding hearts in my garden, and my heart still figuratively bleeds when I see them; I miss her so much, and she's been gone over forty years. (I grew up in a duplex house with my mom and dad and me on one side and my grandparents on the other side.) Even the tulips and pansies in my garden remind me of the tulips and pansies I saw in my grandmother's flower garden when I was a little girl, and I miss my grandmother all over again.

Being an only child, I knew the meaning of being a true orphan.

I have few people to share memories of days with my mom before I met Jim or had children. I have no nieces or nephews, no uncles alive. My only living aunt lives over a thousand miles away. My first-cousins live hundreds of miles away. Perhaps sharing memories would make grief easier, perhaps not.

CHAPTER 8

THE SELF-BLAME

As mentioned before, almost immediately I blamed myself for my mom's death, and I continued to blame myself. Even with the shock of mom's death and the aftermath of the days that were a blur of funeral business—phone calls to notify people of mom's death, making the funeral home arrangements, and preparing for the funeral and the funeral luncheon—I still squeezed in time for self-blame. With each reoccurring memory of the last few days of mom's life, my self-blame intensified. I kept thinking, "**If**," "**If**" "**If**."

LOOKING BACK, to the last Thursday of her life, I thought, *If only I had reminded my mom about her dog when she refused to go to the doctor or emergency room, maybe would have agreed to go to be checked.* When my mom's dog had trouble with her legs a few weeks prior, my mom had been quick to ask me to take her dog to the vet, yet she didn't let me take her to the doctor for her legs. The dog is still alive and well. **If**

only I had gone over to her house on that Thursday, not just offered to take her to the clinic or hospital, maybe I would have remembered about the dog and used that to convince mom to be checked.

LOOKING BACK to the last Friday of her life on earth, **if** I had taken her for chocolate pie that day or at least have sat and had a cup of tea with her, maybe then I would have noticed more about her actions or legs (actually I wouldn't have seen her legs, because she wore slacks at home and to town). **If** we went for that piece of pie, we would have been downtown near the hospital, and I might have talked her into going to the emergency room.

Maybe I **should have** gone home and gotten my reading glasses to check her legs. **If** only I had remembered her legs had been thin, I would have realized she needed to see the doctor. I **should have** remembered that her legs were naturally very thin and may have gotten even thinner over the winter when she began to lose weight. I **should have** spent more time with her after I examined her legs. Maybe **if** I had pressured her, she would have let me take her to the doctor and her heart would have been checked. I **should have** again offered to take her for medical help. (Since I typed this paragraph, I asked my mom's physician's assistant about my mom's legs. I mentioned that I could see her ankles. He said the ankles usually swell when there is a serious problem, and only the calves of the legs swell from a salty meal.)

LOOKING BACK, it seemed strange that "911" were some of the last words I said to her, maybe they were my last words to her. "911" **should have** rung a bell in my brain—maybe her legs were really swollen as they were before her first heart attack. Maybe I realized then that the situation could become serious. However, she looked to be in good health. I didn't change may plans.

I still think of mom standing by her front door the last day I saw her alive—it was our final goodbye on earth, and neither of us knew it. If we had, we would have spent every remaining minute together. Of course, we never did go for that piece of chocolate pie, because she died on Sunday and we were not going to go for the chocolate pie until Monday.

LOOKING BACK, I realized I **could have** asked her to stay at our house overnight, though she always preferred to sleep in her own bed. (She wouldn't even stay at our camp, though she enjoyed being in the woods. She always said she couldn't sleep anywhere except in her own bed.) When her legs had swollen a few years before, I pressured her to stay at our house overnight; she finally agreed, and around six o'clock the next morning, she asked me to take her to the hospital for chest pains. At that time, she was diagnosed with a heart attack and congestive heart failure. She had Lacix medication in an IV to take off the extra water. She had other medications, too. She recovered quickly and returned home from the hospital in a few days. I **should have** insisted that she spend the night at our house, so I'd have heard her if she had pain during the night and convinced her to go to the hospital—maybe she'd even asked me to take her to the hospital as she did before.

I told myself I **should have** broken the promise to my friend to go to the retreat—not put my friend before my mom—and gone to mom's house on Saturday morning and checked her legs.

I told myself I **should have** checked her when I came home from the retreat.

Also, I didn't remember to take time to tell Jim or my son or daughter-in-law to check on her, though the thought had crossed my mind at some time during that Friday; I **should have** asked them to check on her. I did write myself a note reminding me to check on her myself, but I didn't see the note on our kitchen table until the day after we discovered she had died. I **should have** checked on her when I got home from retreat.

[Thankfully (I found out later) my son and his wife did go to visit mom on that Saturday night. Mom told them about her legs and showed them her legs also. Both of them thought her legs weren't swollen and told her that her legs looked okay, but they did not know if her legs had become thinner over the winter. She must have felt fairly well, because she made them a cup of tea, and they said she acted like her usual self.]

Sometimes I went **FURTHER BACK**, remembering ways I neglected to help her. I **could have** raked the collection of dog droppings from around her front porch (those of her dog and from my puppy—she had recently babysat the puppy while we visited one of our sons). I remember she said she probably wouldn't dogsit again. She usually willingly took care of our dogs—even enjoyed it—so we could visit our sons.

Maybe I **should have** realized then that she was slowing down. I **could have** helped her to gather the heavy winter jackets she chose to give away. I **could have** cleared the insulation left in her basement by the home improvement workers I'd found to help her. I **could have** transferred her food from her old refrigerator to her new refrigerator (I wasn't there when the new refrigerator arrived). She had done these chores herself the week she died instead of asking one of us to help or waiting for us to help her as planned.

LOOKING FURTHER BACK, I remembered the doctor had said she was "rattling" when he checked her with a stethoscope during a checkup about a month prior. Neither of us asked him what he meant, and the doctor didn't say, but she said she wondered what he meant. I wondered, too, but I didn't ask him, thinking that his answer might lead mom to worry. Perhaps her congestive heart problem was worsening, and he didn't want to worry her, knowing her tendency to worry a lot. I kept thinking, *If only I had phoned the doctor and asked what he meant by mentioning the rattling in her* chest.

[The death certificate said she died of a heart problem—I didn't understand the medical words. At the reading of the will, I asked the lawyer about the Latin words on the death certificate, and he said they likely meant "heart attack." (No autopsy was performed.) The certificate also said that it took her several hours to die. I hope she didn't feel much pain. She was lying flat, not in a stressful-looking position. (Since I typed this paragraph, I asked my mom's physician's assistant about the matter. He said that if her body wasn't twisted in the bed and if the bedding was smooth, it was likely that she didn't even feel the pain; if in pain, she would have twisted and turned and rumpled the sheets and blankets. Still I wonder if the men, including Jim, who first saw my dead mom had rearranged her or her sheets and blankets. I still don't have the courage to ask.)]

Some people get angry with other people during sorrow, some even get angry with the dead person, because they feel the dead person abandoned them, but I was angry with myself.

I kept thinking, *If I could go back to last Thursday, last Friday, last Saturday. If I could only go back to a week ago, two weeks ago, three weeks ago.* I kept thinking, *If only I had… maybe...."*

I can say, "I could have," "if I would have," "I should have" for the rest of my life, but the "could haves," "would haves," and "should haves" won't bring mom back to earth.

However, I think I will eventually join her in heaven. In the Bible, David had this to say about seeing his dead son again, "But now he is dead, wherefore should I fast? can I bring him back again? I shall go to him, but he shall not return to me." (II Samuel 12:23)

Fasting wouldn't bring back David's son and feeling bad about what I didn't do won't bring back my mom. It makes no difference how much I look back, the past can't be changed. All I can do is keep on living my life for the Lord.

I have the hope of seeing mom in heaven, because I am quite sure she had accepted Christ as her Savior. "We give thanks to God…Since we have heard of your faith in Jesus Christ…For the hope which is laid up for you in heaven, whereof ye heard before in the word of the truth in the gospel…" (Colossians 1:3-5)

Sometimes it might seem that a deceased loved one is not a Christian, has not accepted Jesus in payment for his/her sins, but only God knows what is in another person's heart. "…he knoweth the secrets of the heart." (Psalm 44:21)

Mom was a worrier and often worried that she wasn't saved. To be sure, I went over Scriptures with her and had her repeat a prayer of salvation from one of the books I wrote. I also told her the verses that give God's promise of salvation. "These things have I written unto you that believe on the name of the Son of God; that ye may know that ye have eternal life, and that ye may believe on the name of the Son of God." (I John 5:13)

One day I asked her pastor and a visiting evangelist to visit mom to confirm that she had made a decision; they followed through and told me they were sure she had accepted Jesus. The pastor mentioned that fact in the eulogy he gave at her funeral. "For the hope which is laid up for you in heaven, whereof ye heard before in the word of the truth of the gospel…" (Colossians 1:5) I'll include some of the Scriptures and prayer here for you.

<u>We all sin—nobody is perfect.</u>

"For all have sinned, and come short of the glory of God…" (Romans 3:23)

<u>The good news—the gospel message</u>

"…the gospel…

…how Christ died for our sins according to the scriptures;

And that he was buried, and that he rose again the third day according to the scriptures:

And that he was seen…of above five hundred brethren at once…" (I Corinthians 15:1,3-6)

<u>Only Christ can make us holy enough to go to heaven.</u>

"…the blood of Jesus Christ…cleanseth us from all sin." (I John 1:7)

<u>God has promised us eternal life if we believe in Jesus.</u>

"…what must I do to be saved?

…Believe on the Lord Jesus Christ, and thou shalt be saved…" (Acts 16:30-31)

"…if thou shalt confess with thy mouth the Lord Jesus, and shalt believe in thine heart that God hath raised him from the dead, thou shalt be saved."

(Romans 10:9)

"For God so loved the world, that he gave his only begotten Son, that whosoever believeth in him should not perish, but have everlasting life.

For God sent not his Son into the world to condemn the world; but that the world through him might be saved." (John 3:16-17)

If you believe those words of God, then pray this prayer.

"Dear God,

I agree with Your words in the Bible about salvation.

I admit I am a sinner.

I am sorry I sinned.

I believe that You sent Jesus to die on the cross in payment for my sins.

I believe He rose again and lives in heaven.

I accept Your Gift of Jesus in payment for my sins and for everlasting life with You.

In Jesus' Name, amen.

Your name_____

Today's date_____

If you have prayed this prayer, then I welcome you into the family of God.

"For ye are all the children of God by faith in Christ Jesus." (Galatians 3:26)

CHAPTER 9

THE CONFESSION

I felt like David in the Bible. David knew that his sin had hurt others and had even hurt himself. "I am troubled; I am bowed down greatly; I go mourning all day long. There is no soundness in my flesh…neither is there any rest in my bones because of my sin." (Psalm 38:6,3)

Yes, I could have done more than I did. Maybe I couldn't have gotten mom to go to the hospital, but I could have invited her to stay at our home and I could have checked on her when I returned from retreat—or skipped the retreat.

I knew I couldn't ask mom for her forgiveness, because she was no longer with me. I knew she was no longer alive on earth. I could dial her phone number, but I couldn't talk to her—her phone was disconnected. I could write a letter, but I couldn't mail it to her. I could go to her house, but she wouldn't be home. I could go to her grave and talk, but she wouldn't hear me. In my heart, I knew she would forgive me for any of my neglect of her and love me unconditionally. She would feel bad for my sadness, but not angry.

We all sin, even after we are saved. "If we say that we have no sin, we deceive ourselves…." (I John 1:8) We all tend do things that we should not do, and we sometimes neglect to do what we should do.

When we sin, we need to confess our sins to God, as David did. Remember, our sins really are against God.

> "Have mercy upon me, O God, according to thy lovingkindness: according unto the multitude of thy tender mercies blot out my transgressions.
>
> Wash me thoroughly from mine iniquity, and cleanse me from my sin.
>
> For I acknowledge my transgressions: and my sin is ever before me.
>
> Against thee, thee only, have I sinned, and done this evil in thy sight…" (Psalm 51:1-4)

When we pray the "Lord's Prayer," we also ask God to forgive us our sins. "And forgive us our debts…" (Matthew 6:12)

I confessed what I considered to be my sin of neglecting my mom those last few days of her life.

I knew God had forgiven me, because, in I John 1:9 the Bible says, "If we confess our sins, he is faithful and just to forgive us our sins, and to cleanse us from all unrighteousness."

As David said in the Bible, "I acknowledged my sin unto thee, and mine iniquity have I not hid. I said, I will confess my transgressions unto the Lord; and thou forgavest the iniquity of my sin. Selah." (Psalm 32:5)

Perhaps it was a sin not to forgive myself. I was condemning myself instead of following God's example and forgiving myself as He forgave me. I thought of the verse in the Bible that says, "And be ye kind one to another, tenderhearted, forgiving one another, even as God for Christ's sake hath forgiven you." (Ephesians 4:32) Also, I was wasting precious time God had given me by condemning myself, instead of using the time to serve Him. "Redeeming the time, because the days are evil." (Ephesians 5:16)

God had forgiven me. Mom would have forgiven me. When would I forgive myself**???**

I knew God had forgiven me, but I needed to forgive myself and let my heavy heart be free. I needed to stop wasting time condemning myself and stop telling others what a terrible daughter I was. I needed to be a living example of God's forgiveness. The sooner I forgave myself, the sooner I would be in better condition to continue to go forward for the Lord.

I was familiar with the Scriptures about God's forgiveness, but I kept condemning myself and living by my self-deceit instead of believing God's truths. I was putting confidence in my opinion of myself—guilty, not in the reality of God's promise—forgiven. My self-deceit of "guilty forever" was a convincing lie for me to believe, especially when I told myself the lie over and over and over, embedding the lie deeper and deeper into my brain.

I needed to stop believing my lies, not depend on what I thought to be true, but depend on what God says that is always true.

> "Trust in the Lord with all thine heart; and lean not unto thine own understanding." (Proverbs 3:5)

I needed to trust God Who forgave me. He is wise and always knows what He is doing. God never makes mistakes. I needed to have confidence in His decision to forgive me, even when my conscience condemns me after I have confessed my sin. "For if our heart condemn us, God is greater than our heart, and knoweth all things. Beloved, if our heart condemn us not, then have we confidence toward God." (I John 3:20-21) "It is better to trust in the Lord than to put confidence in man." (Psalm 118:8)

"Trust in the Lord, and do good…" (Psalm 37:3)
When I trusted God's decision to forgive me and decided to forgive myself as He forgave me, I would have more time to serve Him by doing good.

David in the Bible sinned, but he confessed his sin to God and went on to serve God in many ways. I needed to say as David did:
"In thee, O Lord, do I put my trust…"
(Psalm 31:1)

CHAPTER 10

The Insights

The experience of mourning did teach me how to live my life better. I learned some things about myself from my self-examination. "…let a man examine himself…" (I Corinthians 11:28) I see now that, in some ways, I thought I was better than other people.

I thought I was a good listener, better than many people. I think mom had mentioned the possibility of a circulation when she complained about her legs bothering her. She had mentioned for two days that her legs felt swollen, but I wasn't listening well that second day that she complained about her legs. After hearing her complain for two days about her legs (and she seldom complained about them), I could have realized that there was a real problem. I could have listened instead of just gone by what I saw. God gave me good ears. I surely didn't use my ears well those days preceding her death.

Also, I thought I'm an observant person, more observant than most people. However, when I looked at my mom's legs, I didn't stop to think that her legs were unusually thin and had probably become even thinner over the winter when she had begun to lose weight. The water retention had probably plumped up her legs to the size of average legs, but not as her legs usually looked. I surely wasn't observing well those days preceding her death.

Also, I thought I was an understanding person and that I probably had more empathy than most people. I surely didn't relate to how mom felt those last days of her life. I could have said, *"They're your legs. If that's how they feel, then let's have a doctor check on them at the clinic or the emergency room."* I surely didn't empathize with mom that day.

I usually considered myself to be flexible, more flexible than most people, fitting other people into my daily schedule, no matter how busy I was. However, that last Friday mom was alive, I rushed over as soon as she called, checked her legs, and then rushed off to complete my list of things-to-do on my daily schedule. I could easily have spent some extra time with her—had a cup of tea in her kitchen or taken her out for a piece of chocolate pie. I surely wasn't flexible on that Friday.

Also, I had become so busy around that time, that I was spending little time with my family—husband and mom— and more time on running around doing things that were not proper priorities. I should never get in the habit of putting others before my immediate family and becoming so busy that I'm rushing to do more than I should do, to the point of being too busy to take care of myself and to take care of those closest to me. I surely was too busy at that time in my life.

Yes, I thought I was better than other people in those ways, but I should never compare myself with others.

"…Be not wise in your own conceits."
(Romans 12:16)

"Let nothing be done through strife or vainglory…" (Philippians 2:3)

"Pride goeth before destruction, and an haughty spirit before a fall." (Proverbs 16:18)

"Wherefore let him that thinketh he standeth take heed lest he fall." (I Corinthians 10:12)

"For we dare not make ourselves of the number, or compare ourselves with some that commend themselves; but they measuring themselves by themselves, and comparing themselves among themselves, are not wise." (II Corinthians 10:12)

"But he that glorieth, let him glory in the Lord. For not he that commendeth himself is approved, but whom the Lord commendeth." (II Corinthians 10:17-18)

CHAPTER 11

THE WHYS

No matter how wise we are, God is wiser.

I sometimes wish I could go back and relive that Friday, the last day I saw my mom alive. For my sake, I selfishly wish I'd tried harder to help her on that last Friday and Saturday.

For her sake, I'm glad she enjoyed her last days at home on earth instead of in the hospital full of tubes and wires. (I remember my cousins carried their dad—my great-uncle—out of the hospital against the doctor's wishes, because their dad wanted to spend the last days of his life at home.)

My possible plans to have helped my mom the last days on earth were my plans, not God's plans. God plans everything so much better than I do. God knew when my mom would die; I did not. No matter what I did, I could not change God's plans for the date of her death—though, for a long time, I thought I had the power to do just that.

Perhaps God wanted me to go to the retreat to strengthen me for the difficult days ahead. I don't know, but God knows.

Perhaps God wanted mom to die at her home instead of my home to spare me from having the indelible memory of my mom dead in a bed in my home. Perhaps God was protecting me from having the hurt of that constant reminder. I keep telling myself that people usually died in family homes in the past and that people still often die in family homes in the present, yet I know how I react and God knows how I react—he knows me better than anybody, even better than my mom knew me.

Maybe God wanted mom to die at her home, instead of being in a hospital connected to wires and tubes and stressfully worrying about her likely impending death. I knew mom didn't like to sleep in any bed other than her home.

Maybe God wanted her to enjoy her life on earth right to the end, and she did. She got to enjoy a visit from her son and his wife the last Saturday she was alive, even made tea for them.

Forcing mom to go to the hospital would have worried her, and, since it was God's time for her to die, emergency medical help wouldn't have saved her (though, for a long time, I thought it might have saved her). A few house before I typed this, I visited my oldest son, and he said he felt the same way about it. He also believed she was in heaven with her husband and mother.

My mom went right from enjoying her last days on earth at home to enjoying her first days in heaven in God's home, her new home. God's way is best. God's timing is best. God is greater than any person on earth or any creature on earth or in heaven.

Two friends of mom died before her.

One was gentleman who had visited her and taken her to church for many years. He had become terminally ill and died in a nursing home in another city.

One of mom's female friends entered a nursing home quite awhile before mom died. She was confined to a bed for a long time. Mom seldom visited her—it bothered mom to even enter a nursing home to visit. This friend died before mom.

If mom had been confined to a bed in a nursing home because her heart wasn't providing enough oxygen, she would have been extremely unhappy.

Quite awhile before mom died, another of her friends entered a nursing home because of her severe arthritis. She was the sister of the other lady who had been in the nursing home. Once when I went to visit her, she was walking along the hall holding onto a railing. However, her physical health continued to deteriorate. Her mind remained alert. She had always been a lively person, out and about and enjoying being around people and making them laugh. The last time I saw her she was confined to her bed. She was hooked up to a feeding tube. She couldn't walk. Her skin was so thin that she had to have bandages on it to protect it. She trembled. She said she had been in the nursing home for four years.

One of my mom's greatest fears was the possibility of breaking her hip and having to enter a nursing home, even on a temporary basis, until it healed. (She knew I couldn't lift her.) Instead of a nursing home, she is in her heavenly home where she will never fall and break her hip and never be put in a nursing home.

A few weeks after my mom died, her cat died. The vet said the cat had been very sick for over a year, but my mom had wanted to let it live as long as it could.

Within six months after mom died, her two close friends died—Mom on March 20, one friend on May 15, and the other friend (the one in the nursing home) on September 25.

The daughter of one of the friends told me that her mom had mourned a lot when mom died.

Mom was spared the sorrow of the death of two out of four of her friends.

My mom didn't have friends while my dad was alive.

Within a year after my dad died, mom had gained the four friends mentioned. Over the years, these four friends became my friends, too. Sometimes they took me along when they took mom shopping with them. Sometimes I'd take them out when I picked up mom. I took them on woods walks, berry picking, on picnics, out to camp, and shopping. All four of the ladies, including the one who died first, lived on the same short street as mom. When the four friends died, I grieved for all of them.

Over two years after mom died, at our camp one summer morning, I read the Bible, meditated on it, and prayed. We had moved to a smaller house in the spring, and I was so exhausted from downsizing for an auction and moving from one house to another, I had neglected both God and myself.

As I prayed, I thanked God for mom's quick death.

One of her friends had terrible kidney pain before she eventually died. As I mentioned before, three of mom's friends had died in nursing homes. Her mom (my grandmother) had been weak and housebound with Parkinson's Disease and leukemia for close to ten years before her death. My dad and mom's father (my grandfather) had died of cancer. Mom had been spared the effects of a lingering disease.

It might have been easier to accept mom's death if she were severely ill or incapacitated with problems such as arthritis, heart disease, Alzheimer's disease/dementia, stroke, or paralysis. However, such illness would have been harder on mom. I'm thankful she was healthy to the end.

After my prayer of thanksgiving, I felt like a thick gray storm cloud had lifted off my shoulders.

Being at camp, I thought of the big patch of wintergreen plants growing in the woods there. For years after mom died, I felt guilty about eating wintergreen berries when mom was no longer on earth to eat them.

I remembered picking a handful of wintergreen berries for my mom the last fall before she died. The berries were still small and I wondered if mom would be alive to enjoy the wintergreen berries when they plumped up in the spring. Actually, it was strange that such a thought would enter my mind. Had I somehow sensed mom would die before the spring weather arrived? I'm glad she got to enjoy those berries the last fall of her life, even though they were still small then.

Why did my mom die when she did? Why did the circumstances work out the way they did? Why did I not do more for her that Friday I went to check on her?

I realized I could not fathom these "whys."

Perhaps I'll never know the answers to these "whys," but God knows why, and He always has His reasons why He plans what He plans and carries out what He plans.

> "For who hath known the mind of the Lord? or who hath been his counsellor?...how unsearchable are his judgments, and his ways past finding out! For of him, and through him, and to him, are all things: to whom be glory for ever. Amen."
> (Romans 11:34,33,36)

CHAPTER 12

THE SHARING

God sent some people into my life that shared some of their experienced with me and gave me some possible insights into some of the "whys."

A friend from church shared with me how God's timing had been at work with the death of two loved ones in her family. The way things worked out was not what she would have planned, but God had worked it out in a better way than she would have.

At a campers' dinner, a lady shared with me how her mother had died one day while sitting reading a book, and her husband thought she was still alive for many hours, that she had just fallen asleep reading a book. She told me how it was easy on a person to die that way, but harder on the people left behind. We shared how both of our fathers had suffered with terminal cancer before dying. This lady wasn't my real sister, but she was my sister-in-Christ and understood how to comfort me.

stranger at an auction said that it was probably a blessing that my mom, who had congestive heart failure for several years, had died in her sleep, enjoying life right through her last full day on earth. She said a relative of hers had congestive heart failure, but had suffered terribly with breathing problems for the last three years of her life before she died. God can even send a stranger to comfort us in ways He knows are best.

A lady cutting my hair said she saw my mom's obituary in the paper and expressed her sympathy. She said she still constantly misses her mom who had died two years before.

One lady said she knew of another lady who had lost her mother and grandchildren in a house fire.

One friend told me that she was only a teenager when her mom died and that I was blessed to have my mom for so many years.

Another friend shared how she wasn't with her sister-in-law when she died.

Another friend told me how she had chosen to attend college the summer her mom was in a nursing home and had asked her to move near her for the summer; the mother died in the fall. (This friend was married and living in a different state when her mom entered a nursing home.)

"…it is appointed unto men once to die…"
(Hebrews 9:27)

Death is a certain event, and we all go through it, both when others die and when we, ourselves, die.

Dying in your own bed in your own home as my mom did can be a pleasant way to pass.

CHAPTER 13

THE SCRIPTURES

After weeks of sorrow and self-blame, I began to piece things together Scripturally. First of all, God is in control.

GOD CONTROLS CIRCUMSTANCES.

God knew I would see the lady with the badly swollen legs at the chiropractor's office. God knew I would go to the retreat. God knew I would get home late from retreat. God knew the day my mother would die. He could have changed any of the circumstances, but He did not.

Six weeks after my mom's death, a visiting Christian at church preached about Jonah and commented on how God sets up circumstances, even the death of a loved one, to prepare us for His work. God set up the circumstances for Jonah—the storm, the big fish, the withering gourd plant—to prepare Jonah to reach the hearts of the people of Ninevah (Jonah, chapters 1 and 4).

God may have set up the circumstances surrounding my mom's death for His purposes, perhaps for the writing of this chapter of this book, perhaps for writing the entire book.

GOD CONTROLS TIME.

God did love my mom and He still does love my mom. God is in control of life and death, not me. It is God's timing, not mine. God is all-knowing, and He knows the wisest way to make these difficult decisions. God was in control of the date and the time of my mother's death.

God was even in control of the time of the death of His Son, Jesus, a heart-breaking decision for God, the Father, to make. Several times, Jesus escaped imminent death by dangerous people, because His time to die had not yet come. Yet, when the time came for Christ to die, Christ, Himself, could not even choose His time to die.

Only God has the power to control the exact timing of events. "To every thing there is a season…A time to be born, and a time to die…" (Ecclesiastes 3:1-2) As Jesus said, "…It is not for you to know the times or the seasons, which the Father hath put in his own power." (Acts 1:7)

God even knows when a pet dies, even knows when a small animal like a bird dies. Matthew 10:29 says, "Are not two sparrows sold for a farthing? And one of them shall not fall on the ground without your Father."

GOD IS ALL-POWERFUL.

Satan, as powerful as he is, was not allowed to kill Job; God was in control of Job's life.

God let Satan torment Job, but God said to Satan,

> "…save his life." (Job 2:6)

> "There is no man that hath power over the spirit to retain the spirit; neither hath he power in the day of death…" (Ecclesiastes 8:8)

> "Great is our Lord, and of great power: his understanding is infinite." (Psalm 147:5)

> "He ruleth by his power for ever…" (Psalm 66:7)

> As we say when we repeat the Lord's Prayer, "…For thine is kingdom, and the power, and the glory, for ever. Amen."
> (Matthew 6:13)

I NEED TO SUBMIT TO THE WILL OF GOD.

I need to agree with the will of God, not my wants. I wanted mom to live. It was God's will for her to die.

As Jesus said, when He prayed to God the Father in the garden of Gethsemane before His capture and crucifixion,

"...O my Father, if it be possible, let this cup pass from me: nevertheless not as I will, but as thou wilt." (Matthew 26:39)

As Jesus taught the disciples to pray, the prayer most Christians still pray today:

> "...Our Father which art in heaven, Hallowed
> by thy name. Thy kingdom come. Thy will
> be done in earth, as it is in heaven." (Matthew
> 6:9-10)

As we say the "Lord's Prayer," I wonder how often we realize that we are asking God to do what He wants to do, not what we want Him to do.

I have to accept the fact that it was God's will for my mom to die that day.

About seven weeks after the death of my mom, I went out to our backyard to dump soil out of my flowerpots into the flower garden, and I felt terrible, because mom wasn't there to enjoy the warm sunny day. Then I remembered Acts 1:7 (quoted previously in this chapter)—it is God Who controls the times and the seasons..

Most of the people in our area wanted spring to arrive in April, but we had many cold days and snow. Spring finally arrived in May, but it even snowed on the first day of May. We can't determine the seasons.

That was a reminder to me that God not only controls the seasons and the weather, but He also controls the beginning and ending dates of our life—our birth and our death.

We plan for how we will live our lives, but we can't determine the date of our death. In the parable (Luke 12:16-20) of the rich fool who planned to enjoy his riches for many years, "…God said unto him, Thou fool, this night thy soul shall be required of thee…." (verse 20)

I need to remember never to argue with God—not about how He arranges things, not about how He times things. God knows what is best.

The Bible mentions 70 years as the time allotted to us on earth, and 80 being really a lot of time. "The days of our years are threescore years and ten; and if by reason of strength they be fourscore years, yet is their strength labour and sorrow; for it is soon cut off, and we fly away." (Psalm 90:10)

My mom lived to 92, a fact for which I should be grateful, instead of complaining that she didn't live longer, that she didn't live through the spring to which she was looking forward.

"In every thing give thanks: for this is the will of God in Christ Jesus concerning you." (I Thessalonians 5:18)

I am so thankful for having her with me until she was 92 years old.

CHAPTER 14

THE GRIEF

After mom died, I felt like David (in the book of Psalms) and Hezekiah (in the book of Isaiah).

> "I am troubled; I am bowed down greatly; I go mourning all the day long." (Psalm 38:6)

> "I am feeble and sore broken: I have roared by reason of the disquietness of my heart." (Psalm 38:8)

> "Like a crane or a swallow, so did I chatter: I did mourn as a dove: mine eyes fail with looking upward: O Lord, I am oppressed; undertake for me." (Isaiah 38:14)

> "…When wilt thou comfort me?" (Psalm 119:82)

"I am weary with my groaning; all the night make I my bed to swim; I water my couch with my tears.

Mine eye is consumed because of grief…"
(Psalm 6:6-7)

I felt sad like David, but I didn't water my couch or bed with tears. In fact, I've tried not to cry much. Perhaps it's because I keep remembering how my mom used to say, "Don't cry, Mary." That was probably not the main reason I cried little. Perhaps I thought I didn't deserve the luxury of tears after not being with mom the last day she was alive. I think I felt like I didn't deserve to grieve, because I felt like I had neglected mom the last weekend of her life. I think it was part of punishing myself for what I perceived as my neglect of my mom leading to her death. Still, occasionally I burst into tears.

When I do cry, I usually cry in private, but one day our oldest grandson (18 years old) came by and caught me at the end of a crying spell. He comforted me. I felt it should have been me comforting him instead.

Maybe some of us should have cried together at the funeral home when our oldest son cried his heart out, but everyone feels sad at different times and each of us shows our sadness in different ways.

Even Christ cried. John 11:35 is the shortest verse in the Bible, "Jesus wept." It is a short sentence, yet it says so much about the human emotion expressed by crying, an emotion God created in us.

We need to note that Jesus did not cry for selfish reasons or for self-pity. When Jesus wept after His friend, Lazarus died (verse quoted above), it was not for his sadness. Jesus knew He would be raising Lazarus from the dead to live again. He cried about the true sadness for the others who were mourning Lazarus and for their lack of being encouraged by the promise of life in heaven for believers such as Lazarus. Like Jacob, they refused to be comforted.

Jesus also cried for the people of Jerusalem who were lost, because they rejected Him. "And when he was come near, he beheld the city, and wept over it, Saying, If thou hadst known, even thou, at least in this thy day, the things which belong unto thy peace! but now they are hid from thine eyes." (Luke 19:41-42) He knew that the people of Jerusalem would face terrible times in the future (verses 43-44).

My mourning is going on for a long time, like Jacob's sorrow when his sons sold their younger brother, Joseph, into slavery. Jacob "…mourned for his son many days. And all of his sons and all his daughters rose up to comfort him; but he refused to be comforted; and he said, For I will go down into the grave unto my son mourning. Thus his father wept for him." (Genesis 37:34-35)

Somehow I have a page of my medical records of a visit to a physician's assistant two months after mom died. I found the report in my group of notes for this book. Here are a few excerpts from the report.

> "She is in today with a whole list of problems, but her real complaint is that she is under a lot of stress.
>
> Her mother recently died, and she is feeling guilty about not seeing some of the symptoms that led up to her demise and therefore reacting faster and saving her life.
>
> We talked about her mother's death at length, and although her mother was in her 90s, she is probably going to have a little trouble coping with this for a while.
>
> I think through her faith she will probably stabilize."

This understanding person had helped me through trying times in the past, and again he helped me. At that time, I did have health problems, such as needing knee surgery, but the kind P. A. knew what was hurting me most—the loss of my mom—and he patiently listened to me pour out what was on my heart and he encouraged me and guided me.

The grief hit me in many ways.

Someone told me to go to mom's grave, take care of it, talk to her at the grave. I couldn't even go to the cemetery, even though mom and I had put flowers on my grandparents' and great-grandparents' graves every year, starting with the oldest graves when I was a child. Years before, I had put rocks around my granddaughter's grave that had no headstone, but I couldn't decorate mom's who was buried next to that tiny baby girl. Somehow things were different for me with this death. (I've never visited my dog's grave at camp, either—that dog died about a year before mom, so it's been quite awhile. I had never reacted like that to visiting one of my animal's graves before.)

As I mentioned before, I felt like I shouldn't be eating wintergreen berries, because mom couldn't. I felt like I shouldn't enjoy them if mom couldn't. I even felt like I didn't deserve to eat the berries, because I felt responsible for her death.

I felt the same about eating her favorite jam—apricot. I felt like I didn't deserve to enjoy food or flowers or anything else that mom had enjoyed and couldn't enjoy anymore.

I stayed home more, because I felt it wasn't fair for me to go out and have fun with friends when mom couldn't.

I felt guilty doing things she couldn't do anymore, and I felt lonely doing the things we usually did together—shopping, doctor appointments, etc.

Certain stores and restaurants brought back good memories of our times together, but also made me sad, because she could no longer be there.

I couldn't even bear to look at items I'd bought when we had shopped together.

I didn't even wear the jacket I had bought months before her death, because it matched the one I had given mom for Christmas. Likewise, though I wanted to give my jacket to a friend I knew who would like it, I didn't give it away, because I knew I'd still see it again and be sad.

I couldn't bear to look at gifts she had given me or use the silverware she had used at my home. I couldn't sit in the rocker she had rocked at our camp.

I couldn't bear to go to her house, even though I now owned it.

Yes, I still mourn for my mom, and sometimes I cry when I see something that reminds me of her and I start to miss my her again, but mom can't mourn for being apart from me or cry or worry or be afraid, because all is well with her in heaven.

"And God shall wipe away all tears from their eyes; and there shall be no more death, neither sorrow, nor crying, neither shall there be any more pain: for the former things are passed away." (Revelation 21:4)

Mom no longer has a fear of heights, though she's high in the sky in heaven. She is safe forever, no more pain in her heart, no more car accidents, not even a mosquito bite. (You can tell, by the time I type this book a second time, my sense of humor has returned.) Mom now knows she won't have to play a harp or wear wings, as she feared while she was on earth. She has seen that only the angels have wings, not the people.

Heaven is a happy peaceful place where people don't try to force you to do what you don't want to do, such as play a harp. If any people play the harp, it will because they like to play the harp or because they want to do it to please God, Who likes music.

> "O death, where is thy sting? O grave, where is thy victory?
>
> ...thanks be to God, which giveth us the victory through our Lord Jesus Christ." (I Corinthians 15:55,57)

God took the sting of death away from my mom and gave me hope knowing I will see her again in heaven.

Yet, I do still mourn for her, but God is guiding me through the grief.

> "The Lord had heard my supplication; the Lord will receive my prayer." (Psalm 6:9)
>
> "O Lord my God, in thee do I put my trust..." (Psalm 7:1)

CHAPTER 15

THE RESOLUTION

For a long time, guilt went along with my grief. Guilt dragged me down. I wasted time I could have spent serving God. I stayed away nights reliving those last few days mom was alive, condemning myself. Then I was tired in the morning—too tired to concentrate, sometimes too tired to work, too tired to serve God.

The guilt compounded my grief and delayed my mourning. I even felt like I did not deserve to grieve, that I did not have the right to grieve.

I went down, down, down.
It was somewhat like this.

Death
↓
Grief
↓

Guilt
↓
Discouragement
↓
Depression

Years ago, I put one foot into quicksand and quickly backed up. Now I need to back away from condemning myself or the quicksand of self-condemnation will pull me down into depression. With God, I can surface from past sins—both imagined sins and real sins.

Here are some of answers when we sink down with a discouraging problem

> TALK TO GOD.
> "Save me, O God; for the waters are come in unto my soul.
>
> I sink in deep mire, where there is no standing: I am come into deep waters, where the floods overflow me.
>
> I am weary of my crying: my throat is dried: mine eyes fail while I wait for my God.

Deliver me out of the mire, and let me not sink: let me be delivered…out of the deep waters.

Let not the waterflood overflow me, neither let the deep swallow me up, and let not the pit shut her mouth upon me." (Psalm 69:1-3,14-15)

WAIT FOR GOD TO ANSWER YOUR PRAYER.

"I waited patiently for the Lord; and he inclined unto me, and heard my cry.

He brought me up also out of an horrible pit, out of the miry clay, and set my feet upon a rock, and established my goings.

And he hath put a new song in my mouth, even praise unto our God: many shall see it, and fear, and shall trust in the Lord.

Blessed is the man that maketh the Lord his trust…"

(Psalm 40:1-4)

I am making progress in setting aside my overwhelming sorrow and going forward for the Lord.

"…Jesus said…Follow me; and let the dead bury their dead." (Matthew 8:22) "He that loveth father or mother more than me is not worthy of me…" (Matthew 10:37) "And whosoever doth not bear his cross, and come after me, cannot be my disciple." (Luke 14:27)

Yes, I will continue to miss my mom and feel sorrow, but I will not let sorrow be the controlling factor of my life.

I am also making progress in dealing with my self-blame.

A friend (the one who stuck with me the week of the funeral) called me a few days ago, and I told how I lay awake night after night, still thinking about how I could have helped my mom more the last few days of her life. I think about those last three days she was alive and the day of her death when I go to bed, and I wake up every few hours during the night thinking about those four days, I wake up in the morning thinking about those four days—what I could have done better.

My friend said God wouldn't send me those terrible thought, but Satan does. Satan wants to hurt me. My friend reminded me that Satan does not want me to continue my book ministry for God.

My friend's wise words helped me realize that, although I suffered much from self-blame for my mom's death, my book ministry also suffered from my self-blame. I wasted God's gift of time by this futile mental self-flagellation.

Paul, in the Bible, did things that displeased God. Paul even hurt Christians before he became a Christian, himself, but he did not continually waste time whipping himself with self-blame. He went forward and served God.

With my friend's help, I finally realized that Satan is trying to deceive me, to discourage me so much that I no longer have strength to serve God. Satan wants me to waste time on self-blame, to lose sleep on self-blame, and be too tired to serve God.

God wants me to sort out the lies about self-blame that I was believing about myself and rediscover His true words in the Bible and apply those truths to my life.

God wants me to use my time wisely, probably to finish the typing of this book to bring Him glory and to guide people to Jesus and help people climb out of the grave of grief. "For we are his workmanship, created in Christ Jesus into good works, which God hath before ordained that we should walk in them." (Ephesians 2:10)

Today, the day I'm typing this page, I woke up with those terrible thoughts again, but this time, I turned to my Bible. I remembered that I have to combat Satan's lies with God's Scriptures which are always true. I realized I have to replace the old hurtful lies about mom's death with helpful Scriptures, so Satan won't have room to step back in and deceive me. These were the Scriptures that came to me.

"…discern both good and evil." (Hebrews 5:14)

"…put off…the old man…
…put on the new man…
Neither give place to the devil."
(Ephesians 4:22,24,27)

"Beloved, believe not every spirit, but try the spirits whether they are of God…

Hereby know ye the Spirit of God: Every spirit that confesseth that Jesus Christ is come in the flesh is of God:

And every spirit that confesseth not that Jesus Christ is come in the flesh is not of God…

Ye are of God, little children, and have overcome them: because greater is he that is in you, than he that is in the world." (I John 4:1-4)

I need to continually recognize Satan's lies in my life and put off the lies and put on God's truths, so Satan won't have a space in my mind to plant his lies. I have to remember that God is greater than Satan, and I am a child of God, so God is on my side in my battle against the deceit of the devil.

I not only have to listen to God's Word in the Bible, but talk to Him, keep going to Him in prayer—talk over my problems with Him and ask for His help and accept His help.

I knew I had to quit punishing myself with self-blame, and, instead of wasting time regretting, I needed to use the time God gave me for serving Him.

One thing I did with this precious God-given time was to finish writing this short "self-help with God" book, <u>Death of a Mother</u>, to help people who were suffering with sorrow of a death or self-blame for a death.

Each of us should wisely use the time God gives us.

None of us should waste time giving false blame to ourselves or accepting false blame from others.

Note: The death of the author's father is included in the author's book, <u>Woman in the Well</u>, a true story to help people who are depressed. The author was falsely blamed for the death of her father whom she helped to battle cancer. Many daily living situations are covered in the book.

CHAPTER 16

THE SPECIAL HELP
FROM PEOPLE

A Note to You, the Reader

As I set out to write this book, I cautioned myself to keep all the chapters short, because grieving people might be experiencing fatigue. Originally there were only 16 chapters in this book, not 18.

However, a computer repair shop lost two of my computers that had 12 books in them, about 3,000 pages. Some of the old floppies seem to be usable (they haven't all been checked out yet), but at least two floppies were blank—this book and <u>Woman in the Well</u>, the two books that were, emotionally, the most hard for me to write.

Now, six years later, I'm updating the printout of this book. Because of that, I'm reliving those dreadful days after the death of my mom.

However, some good has come out of this—I added two chapters to the book. The last three chapters might be longer than the others, but I think that is good, because these chapters are uplifting and full of positive solutions to the situations that often accompany death.

These chapters demonstrate two Scriptures. "And we know that all things work together for good to them that love God, to them who are the called according to his purpose." (Romans 8:28) "…with God all things are possible." (Matthew 19:26) Instead of the book ending on a sad note and with many parts of my mourning unresolved, the book has a happy ending.

As I mentioned in this book, with the help of many people, I managed to cope in the days immediately following mom's death, but it took a long time to recover from the intense sorrow. With help from God, Scriptures, and the many people God brought into my life, I slowly recovered.

I've devoted this chapter to a few specific ways a few people helped me with my grief during the first six months after mom's death. These people are not more important than other people who helped me, but I'm including more details in this chapter, going in further depth than before.

At 2 months later, a pastor in Pennsylvania

At 5 months later, a speaker at a retreat

At 6 months later, a letter from a friend

—2 months after mom died—

Two months after mom's death, Jim and I took his mom and one of his brothers to visit Jim's family.

One of the main reasons for the trip was that Jim's mom wanted to visit her last remaining sister-in-law; all the other relatives of that generation had already passed. The two elderly ladies wept with joy at seeing each other.

We visited cemeteries to look for graves of their ancestors and visit more recent family graves. The tombstones brought back memories of Jim's relatives whom I had met that were buried there and memories of mom in her new grave.

At one stop, Jim's mom and brother went in a store and Jim waited in the van. I went to a church across the street to drop off my book coupon with the eight steps to travel to success. I hand out these coupons where I travel, both to market my book and to help people find Jesus and be a godly success. At this church, though, I received help as well as gave help.

I wandered though the beautiful old white frame church in search of an office. I found the pastor in his office and gave him my book sample.

While talking to the pastor about my books, I suddenly brought up the death of my mother and my feelings of guilt for her death—I had no plans of doing that when I entered the office.

This young, but wise, pastor listened to me and made a few comments. He shared how, when his father was in the hospital, the father told his other son (the pastor's brother) to go on his vacation as planned. Then the father died unexpectedly while the son was gone—similar to my leaving my mom to go to the retreat.

This young pastor was a fine Christian, mature beyond his years. I wanted to visit with him longer, because he had such godly wisdom, but I knew pastors are often very busy and I knew Jim was waiting in the van, so I said I'd have to leave.

As I turned to the door and was leaving the pastor's office, he asked me, "Who is the judge? You?"

That question stopped me in my tracks. I realized I was trying to usurp God's position as judge of how I cared for me mom.

I humbly replied to the pastor's question with a "No. God is."

When I got home from the trip, I looked up verses on God being our judge. As Psalm 50:6 states, "…God is judge himself…." Paul said in I Corinthians 4:3-5, "…I judge not mine own self…but he that judgeth me is the Lord. Therefore, judge nothing before the time, until the Lord come…."

I have no right to judge others or judge myself. Only God has that right.

Yes, we are supposed to look at our behavior and determine if it is bad or good. "…let a man examine himself…" (I Corinthians 11:28)

Yes, we are supposed to confess our bad behaviors.

However, we are not supposed to judge ourselves and condemn ourselves and punish ourselves, and we are not supposed to accept judgment and condemnation by others. Those decisions are God's. (God did provide the court system to handle crimes, but that is different than individual personal judgments.)

Almost a thousand miles from home, God brought a stranger into my life to help me. I was thankful to God for leading me to that wise young pastor to counsel me in my time of need.

God's truths work; His truths even help us deal with false blame. We need to replace unjust blame with God's truths.

—5 months after mom died—

A few months after returning from Pennsylvania, I went to a ladies' retreat about a hundred miles from my home.

It was a bit hard going to retreat, because the day before the previous spring retreat was the last day I saw my mom alive. To top things off, my mom had died a few hours after the day I returned from that spring retreat.

Also, during the last three fall retreats, during each retreat, one of my cousins had died and was buried during the two and one-half days I was at retreat. I'm not superstitious, but these four sad losses were on my mind.

(Note: As I retype this information six years after I first wrote it, I think perhaps God was sparing the sorrow of attending the funerals of those three cousins. Perhaps He also wanted me to go to spring retreat mentioned here to help me rest and rejuvenate and gain strength to face mom's death and funeral.)

The first two days of retreat were terrific. On the second day, the speaker said that God's job is to be the judge, and our job is to be merciful.

I knew I showed mercy to others, but that statement by the retreat speaker helped me to realize I also needed to show mercy to myself and not condemn myself. (It was similar to the insight given to me by the pastor in Pennsylvania.)

I had continued to condemn myself all those months since my mom died. Sometimes I reached the point of self-abuse and hit myself for self-punishment as I had sometimes done in the past.

When going to the small-group prayer session the next morning, I planned to encourage others to give their prayer requests. I had given my requests at a previous meeting and I wanted to give the other ladies plenty of time to talk and express their prayer requests.

Early in the prayer meeting, the leader asked us what we learned—how we were helped—by what the speaker said. After a few ladies spoke, there was a moment of silence, and I impulsively decided to say how the speaker's words on God's judgment and our mercy helped me, hoping what I said would help others. I mentioned how I realized that I also have to be merciful to myself.

However, then I began to open up more and more and more about my sorrow, my self-blame.

If I had briefly mentioned that information, all would have gone well, but, as I spoke, I unintentionally became emotional. Faster and faster and faster I was getting flashbacks—bad memories of looking at my mom's legs, breaking into her house and discovering her body, noticing the vomit running down her mouth, and seeing her in the coffin. I had no prior plan to pour out what was breaking my heart, but my Post-traumatic Stress Disorder kicked in, a problem I had battled for many years.

The prayer group leader reminded me about the workshop on the sovereignty of God—how God is in control, even of when and where and how my mom died. She was very helpful.

Then the group leader said that our limited prayer time was passing and that it was time to stop talking and pray. She said that some people took up too much of the prayer time.

I knew in my head that she was right, but my emotions were reeling out of control, and I felt like I was left dangling, hurting. I started wondering why the ladies weren't reaching out to me and showing me the compassion the retreat speaker had stressed so much. I needed words and hugs of comfort. My tears began to flow. I apologized for taking up too much time. I got up and left, saying I wouldn't take up any more of their time. They asked me to stay, but I walked out.

I felt my emotional level dropping fast as I walked back to the cabin. I knew I had packed a few pills of a strong medication prescribed for Post-traumatic Stress emergency times. (In addition, I was already on a milder daily prescription.) I knew I could ward off a full-blown stress attack if I took an emergency pill.

One friend was at the cabin and asked if I was O.K. I said I was going for a walk. I took a pill and headed out for a walk.

Another friend had returned to the cabin and she asked if I was O.K., and I told her I was going for a walk to Lake Superior (it's near the camp).

On the way, I decided to look for rocks on the beach with bits of blue in them (blue is my favorite color), but then I realized that the rocks with blue would simply remind me of how blue I was feeling when I took the walk.

On the way to the beach, as I was walking along the path through the woods, I saw a dead tree, barren of bark, and thought it was like me, stripped to my soul and left alone. (I knew bears roamed that woods, but my disturbing emotions won out over my fear of bears.)

I also thought of how unready I was to speak to others. I realized that the incident may have been a reminder that I was not emotionally ready to speak. It seemed that God then said that He had called me to be a writer, not a speaker. (Time will tell what plans God has for me later on.)

Walking the beach, I found a fossil of a shell, and it reminded me that God is everlasting—always there from the beginning and forever. God was here before the fossils. God will be here after the fossils are gone. "Jesus Christ the same yesterday, and to day, and for ever." (Hebrews 13:8) I held tightly to that fossil for the rest of the walk, and then put it in my pocket the rest of the day as a reminder that God was with me all the way. Hebrews 13:5 says that God said, "…I will never leave thee, nor forsake thee." Not only is God everlasting, but He always loves us. "…I have loved thee with an everlasting love…" (Jeremiah 31:3) That verse reminded me that all I need is God, not people.

Later I felt bad about the prayer group incident. Because of my emotional story, I unintentionally had the prayer leader "steal time" from the prayer meeting to ask me questions and give counsel. By talking so much, I had unintentionally stolen prayer request time from the other ladies. I felt badly because I had disrupted the prayer meeting and maybe hurt young Christians or unbelievers. I prayed that my leaving the meeting wouldn't hurt others or discourage them.

I also thought about other things I had done at the prayer meeting. I had silently condemned the prayer group ladies for not showing me compassion. The main speaker had said how important it was to be compassionate. However, in forming this opinion of the ladies, I wasn't compassionate. I had been judgmental, taking over God's job of judging—just what the retreat speaker had told us <u>not</u> to do. God is the only judge. I did not know the hearts of those ladies. Only God knows what is in the heart.

The retreat speaker had also admonished us to be merciful. I was not merciful to those ladies in the prayer group.

At lunch time, the prayer leader came up to me and apologized for the wording of what she said. She said the other ladies said they had talked quite a lot at the prayer session, not only me. She hugged me.

At church on Sunday, I received more Scripture that I needed. Timothy must have felt like I felt at the prayer meeting when he said, "...all men forsook me......" (II Timothy 4:16) The following verse is, "...the Lord stood with me...." (II Timothy 4:17)

As I write this, it's about six months since mom died. I'm not yet healed. **In God's time**, I remind myself.

Meanwhile, I'm getting more and more godly insights.

One such insight is this: we need to search our conscience so we know what to confess to God, but we should not judge ourselves or anyone else. (That was similar to the information the pastor in Pennsylvania gave me, but I still needed to hear it again and again and again.)

Another insight is: we should be merciful (not self-condemn) to ourselves and merciful (not condemn) to others.

Simply put these insights are:

> Be compassionate,
> merciful,
> non-judgmental
> to others
> <u>and</u>
> to yourself.

—6 six months after mom died—

About six months after mom died, a friend sent me a letter regarding death from congestive heart failure. Because he knew that I had been thinking I could have prevented mom's death, he said he remembered some similar deaths. His two aunts had died of congestive heart failure in nursing homes and the trained staff could do nothing to prevent the deaths.

A friend of his had a heart attack while at a doctor's office having an examination; the doctor was right there and couldn't do anything to save him. The person who wrote the letter said he hoped his thoughts would help me out a bit, but he knew how hard it is to let go of our ideas and how we feel. People say to "let go," but it's easier to say than do. He said our thoughts aren't always as rational as they should be. He agreed with me that it's hard to forgive ourselves. He said it's easier to forgive others.

I appreciated the letter and the thought that went into it. The medical facts helped me think sensibly, but remnants of guilt kept popping up. A word, a newspaper report, even seeing pie listed on a menu could set off the thoughts of self-blame. Guilt and grief often team up and battle against self-forgiveness.

—12 months after mom died—

A year after mom's death, I almost didn't go to the spring retreat, because I was still dwelling on the death of mom that had occurred on the first day of spring—the day after I had returned from the spring retreat.

Then I listened to an insightful Bible study at church.

I don't have detailed notes and Bible quotations of this study, but what the teacher said had a positive impact on me, and I applied the Scriptures he quoted.

I put in my reservation for the retreat.

"Where no counsel is, the people fall: but in the multitude of counselors there is safety." (Proverbs 11:14)

CHAPTER 17

THE GOOD MEMORIES

Memories can be bad, sad, or glad. For a long time, the bad and sad memories of my mom outnumbered the glad memories.

Sometimes something sets off both good and bad memories.

Sunflowers are a symbol of both sad and glad memories for me. Seeing a sunflower reminded me of the sunflower curtains in mom's dining room where we had many holiday meals— glad memories. However, after mom's first heart attack, Jim and I turned that room into a downstairs bedroom for mom, and I got her a sunflower bedspread. She died in that bed—a sad memory.

However, one by one, the glad memories arrived.

Mom died in March at age 92, and I sure wasn't used to her being gone. However, that same month, as mentioned before, we received another grandson, Suthin, and that helped a lot—a new addition to our family. As Job said in chapter 1, verse 21, "…the Lord gave, and the Lord hath taken away; blessed be the name of the Lord." God took mom, but gave us Suthin.

For many months, I felt bad, especially because I had no brothers or sisters with whom to grieve and remember my childhood with mom. Then one Sunday in church, the congregation sang, "Jesus Is All the World to Me." I realized Jesus was there with mom and me during my childhood, and He remembers my childhood, so I can talk over my childhood memories with Him.

Then the pastor said that Jesus is like an "elder brother." I have a brother after all.

Other hymns sung that day gave the message that Jesus is also our Best Friend, so I have a Best Friend from my childhood, too—a Best Friend yesterday, today, and forever. The hymns were: "I've Found a Friend," "What a Friend We Have in Jesus," and "Turn Your Eyes upon Jesus."

The day of that church service was four months—almost to the day—from when mom died.

Still, though, sad memories popped up—over and over again.

Mom died on the first official day of spring, but spring weather didn't arrive until many weeks later. When I saw a hyacinth coming up in my garden, I remembered my mom had given it to me, and I began to miss her all over again.

In a nearby town, I saw a hill covered with daffodils and thought of the funeral flowers—both mom's and dad's.

When I saw the birch tree outside our bedroom window in the morning, I remembered it was mom who told me where to find it in the woods near her house, so Jim could dig it up and bring it home. It was like a small bush back then. Now it is tall and birds sit on its high branches by our second-floor bedroom window.

When I saw the cedar bushes outside the kitchen window, I'd remember how mom had found them discarded at a cemetery and told me about them, so I could pick them up and plant them in my garden.

I sort of lived in a state of expectancy, waiting for morning phone calls that never came. I knew her phone was disconnected, but I was in the habit of answering her phone calls every morning around ten o'clock as well as at other times during the day.

When the phone did ring, I'd think it was my mom calling. She had called almost every day for about forty years, sometimes many times a day, especially for about the twenty-five years since my dad had died. I also called her.

I'd still expect to make the appointment for her annual checkup in August and her six-month checkup with a skin specialist. (We always went to the same doctor together to have growths burned off and then have a muffin at the hospital snack bar.)

When I saw the dog mom had bought me as a puppy the year before she died, I'd think of mom.

When I went to her favorite restaurant that sells chocolate pie, I would think of her.

When I'd go to a store where we shopped together, I'd think of her.

I even stored my shirt I bought when I was with her, because it reminded me of what I think of as our last shopping trip together. The memory of that shopping trip is a good memory, but sometimes even good memories hurt. I almost didn't buy that shirt for myself that day a few weeks before she died, because I knew she was getting older, and I knew if she died, the shirt would remind me of her. That same day, I almost bought a large seashell for my shell collection, but I didn't, knowing that seeing it would remind me of her if she died ahead of me. Somehow, those thoughts had entered my mind less than two weeks before she died, and, at the time of those thoughts, my mom was alive and well and enjoying the shopping trip. I wonder if those thoughts were a premonition, a way God was preparing me for mom's death in the near future.

All the memories aren't selfishly about my feelings. Some of the reminders of memories make me think about how much I want my mom to be still on earth enjoying things she so much enjoyed, especially the signs of spring that arrived soon after she died on the first day of spring—the honking Canadian geese flying north in the spring, the chirping of the robins, the peeping of the frogs, the first dandelion to bloom.

I realize I won't be taking her on her annual spring woods walk to pick spring beauties, yellow and purple violets, and cowslips. (I recall our walk to her favorite frog pond last spring. I also remember a walk in the fall when she had chest pains and couldn't finish the walk—a first for her—and our youngest son ran full speed to get my four-wheel drive vehicle to rescue her out of the woods. That day she refused to be checked at the hospital.)

I remind myself that she might be enjoying all these things in heaven. After all, God did create them on earth, and He does give us all good things, both on earth and in heaven. Perhaps it's always springtime in heaven. Perhaps there's snow in some parts of heaven for those who like snow and colorful autumn leaves for those who enjoy fall colors.

People had warned me that special days would be really hard the first year—Mother's Day, her May birthday, Memorial day, the first Thanksgiving without her, the first Christmas without her, Palm Sunday (she had died on Palm Sunday), and the anniversary of the day of her death (the first day of spring, as mentioned before). In mom's case, three of those special days are in May.

Less than two months after mom died, Mother's Day was approaching. There were ads for Mother's Day gifts on television, there were Mother's Day cards in stores. There were flowers and candy for sale for Mother's Day.

Every year there is a Mother-Daughter luncheon at our church and usually mom went with me. This year I didn't go. I wasn't ready. The luncheon invitation always included any daughter (in other words, any girl or lady, because all females are the daughter of somebody), so, with or without a mother, any female of any age could attend. That is a kind way to invite people—no female, such as me with three sons, is left out of the luncheon. (The men work in the kitchen and serve at the tables that day. They sometimes have a Father's Day breakfast/ brunch with the ladies working in the kitchen.)

At church on Mother's Day, there were hymns sung about mothers. Also at church, there were printed invitations for all ladies for the upcoming Mother-Daughter luncheon as well as announcements during the church service.

After church, ladies were given carnations—red if your mom was alive, pink if you liked the color, and white if your mother was deceased. I chose a pink flower and left it near the door of my daughter-in-law's home on the way back from church. I had been neglecting myself and was too dizzy to climb the stairs to the apartment there. I'd almost passed out at church and someone there asked me if I'd changed my medications lately. I remembered I hadn't been taking my potassium. I went home and took the prescribed potassium.

However, God's timing was at work again. When I got home from church on Mother's Day, Jim showed me a section of the Sunday paper. There was a half-page book review of one of my novels, <u>Raging Fire</u>. It included the book cover in color and was full of excellent comments about my book. This was my first book review printed in our local paper, the first time that one of my books was publicly acknowledged. I had waited years for that to happen. I think God must have timed it to provide a happy happening in my life on Mother's Day.

Jim sent the book review via computer e-mail to several relatives and friends. I began to receive wonderful note of congratulations, even from Europe. This is one of the e-mails.

> *Dear Mary,*
>
> *The write-up about your book in The Mining Journal is great—neat that it was in the paper on Mother's Day.*
>
> *Mary, I know your mom is looking down from heaven and is smiling and as happy for you as I am.*

I knew mom's birth date, May 21, would be hard for me. However, as already mentioned, our middle son and his wife adopted a boy, Suthin, about the same time my mom died. He was born on May 21 in Thailand, almost six years before he was adopted. (God knew that, too.)

It seems so amazing that Suthin's birthday is the same day as mom's. I guess I shouldn't be surprised—God works things out in His wonderful ways, and, when we're down, He knows how to lift us up.

On May 21, Jim and I were in Pennsylvania celebrating our new grandson's sixth birthday. Mom never got to meet this great grandson, but I didn't have much time for sadness on that day, because our new grandson was so full of life and laughter and fully enjoying his birthday. Again, God worked out another milestone in my grief.

Our middle son and his wife also have a daughter, Sorya, who was born in April. It helps to look forward with happiness to these spring birthdays instead of sadly remembering mom's birthday.

I know I still have to face the first Christmas and the first day of spring without mom, but God will take me through those days.

UPDATE

As I re-type this book, I can update this chapter. I can tell you that God took me through the first Christmas.

In February, almost a year after mom died, I heard people talking about the first day of spring coming soon.

As I mentioned before, mom died on the first day of spring, and, for the first time in me life, I didn't look forward to the first day of spring.

When I got to church that spring day, in my mailbox at church, there was a card of encouragement from a friend. She added a personal note on the card.

May God's love turn your mourning into memories of joy, this year anniversary of your mom's passing.

She had added a sticker that said: "With joy you will draw water from the wells of salvation. Isaiah 12:3"

The card itself had a Scripture quote: "…I have remembrance of thee in my prayers…" II Timothy 1:3 KJV I'm sure this friend was praying for me, especially that weekend.

The sad memories remained, but glad memories arrived as well.

I remembered the photo of mom holding me when I was a baby.

I remembered mom taught me the children's prayer— "Now I lay me down to sleep, I pray the Lord my soul to keep, If I should die before I wake, I pray the Lord me soul to take."

I remembered the doll clothes she made me, especially the red tam and cape.

I remembered the clothes she sewed for me, even a tailored winter white blazer and a yellow concert dress with a scalloped waistline (a complicated pattern I chose). I remembered the shrimp salad she made for my dinner the night of a concert, because the vocalists were supposed to eat light food. I remember her selling her dining room set to my grandmother, so she could buy me a piano. I remember her singing as she ironed. I remember my mom, dad, and me singing in the car—the songs of the era when they were teens and young adults, decades before I was born (not quite the current songs), but I learned them and enjoyed them. I remembered our talks and our walks.

I remember picking flowers every spring near a frog pond. I remember us picking wild apples in the woods in that same area in the fall.

I remember driving my mom to get a Persian cat, and then, at her suggestion, we went to a farm where there were kittens. The farmer had a little barn full of cats and kittens of all colors. I wanted a kitten with extra toes. By the time the farmer found that kitten, most of the cats and kittens had escaped from the barn. The farmer had rounded them all up to be picked up by someone that day, but he wasn't perturbed that his work was in vain. He was a really a patient good-natured person.

I remember taking my mom of a ride and we stopped at a pond full of white water lilies. I took photos of her and the lilies.

I remember taking mom to an "almost-an-island" park where I took nature photos and we enjoyed double-dip ice cream cones. She was around 90 years old then. I snapped a quick photo of her eating the ice cream cone. She wasn't pleased with the surprise photo, but I prefer natural pictures to planned poses, and that photo captured that fond memory of her.

More and more glad memories returned.

Eventually, I was even able to remember her coming to our home for Christmas dinners.

At an authors' book signing at our local library, I met other authors and talked to people interested in my books. Mom came and I have a photo of us together there. I included this photo on the back cover of this book, memorializing a good memory.

As always, God's Word rings true. "…weeping may endure for a night, but joy cometh in the morning." (Psalm 30:5) My night of mourning was slowly coming to an end.

Some of the memories that had made me sad were finally making me glad. The glad memories were outweighing the sad memories. I was at last enjoying the joy of good memories

The hole in my heart was healing; it was filling with good memories of the things mom and I did together.

CHAPTER 18

THE PROGRESS REPORT — 6 YEARS LATER

Recovery from my mom's death did not happen all at once. Even after I knew both the medical and Biblical facts, it took quite a long time for me to assimilate them. It was a lengthy process, but progress was gradually made.

I made notes on some of the incidents. Some incidents I did not journal.

These journal entries are not in chronological order, but sorted according to content.

November 16, the year my mom had died
>
> I heard thunder during the snowstorm.
>
> That reminded me that God is in control. No matter what we do or don't do, God is still in final control. No matter what mistakes

we make, God can choose the final results. Sometimes He allows bad things to happen, as with my dog and mom.

Still, He is omnipotent—in control of all creation.

April 19, over a year after my mom died

Tonight I gave a quick cry to God for help. I again had begun to blame myself for her death. God's words in the Bible came to me—"Be still…" (my child) "and know that I am God." Somehow the words, "my child," got added as I remembered the quote. It was as if God was speaking to me. It was a real reminder to me—God is in control, not me. I looked up the exact quote. "Be still, and know that I am God…" (Psalm 46:10)

June 12, two years after my mom died

I heard on Christian radio that God doesn't want us to be sad. The book of Philippians has a lot to say about joy and rejoicing. I've found that it can be uplifting going through the four chapters of Philippians (it's only a few pages long in all) and underlining the words "joy" and "rejoice." Paul the author of that book of the Bible, went through terrible troubles, but yet he knew the value of joy. In

Philippians 4:4, Paul reminds up to rejoice. "Rejoice in the Lord alway: and again I say, Rejoice." Even in jail, with his feet held in stock, Paul sang. "And at midnight Paul and Silas prayed, and sang praises unto God: and the prisoners heard them." (Acts16:25) Our joy can lift the spirits of others and help turn their sadness into gladness. One of my favorite verses in the Bible is Psalm 118:24. "This is the day which the Lord hath made; we will rejoice and be glad in it." Every day can be a glad day with God. Gladness and joy go with being thankful and trusting in God. "In every thing give thanks: for this is the will of God in Christ Jesus concerning you." (I Thessalonians 5:17) "O give thanks unto the Lord; for he is good..." (Psalm 136:1) "Trust in the Lord..." (Psalm 37:3) "Praise ye the Lord..." (Psalm 147:1) "...and again I say, Rejoice." (Philippians 4:4)

September, two years after my mom died

I was feeling down about mom's death, and Jim said I had brought joy into her life. I'd never thought about that, but I guess I did bring her joy for many many years. It is a comfort knowing that now.

February 12, almost seven years after mom died

I've been retyping this chapter. In church this morning, I read in the book of Job that says God is in control of winds, water, rain, lightning, thunder.

> "To make the weight for the winds; and he weigheth the waters by measure.
> When he made a decree for the rain, and a way for the lightning of the thunder…" (Job 28:25-26)

With all this power, how can God not be in charge of death? God does control death.

Over these past six years, more and more I realize that God is in control.

> "For he commandeth, and raiseth the stormy wind, which lifteth up the waves thereof." (Psalm 107:25)

> "He maketh the storm a calm, so that the waves thereof are still." (Psalm 107:29)

God is in control. Only God can give life. Only God can take life. "…It is not for you to know the times or the seasons, which the Father hath put in his own power." (Acts 1:7)

Satan could tempt Job and make trouble for Job, but could not kill Job. "And the Lord said unto Satan, Behold, he is in thine hand; but save his life." (Job 2:6) Job went through hard times, but he knew God was in control. Job said, "...the Lord gave, and the Lord hath taken away; blessed be the name of the Lord." (Job 1:21) Job's children had just died, but Job still praised God. In Job, chapter 42, the last chapter of the book of Job, it says that Job had ten more children and lived to see four generations. Like Job, we should recognize that God is in control and keep praising God and thanking God.

November 5, nine months after mom died

> During Job's troubled time, he knew God's powerful position. Jeremiah knew God's power.

>> God "Who giveth rain upon the earth..." (Job 5:10)
>> God "...maketh lightnings with rain..." (Jeremiah 51:16)

<hr/>

February 5, two years after mom died

> Two years after my mom died, I got more insight into God's control. If we could control death, most people who are dead would still be alive, because we don't want our loved ones to leave us. Also, since most people do not want to die, most dead people would still

be alive, because it is likely they would have chosen to keep themselves alive.

God is so much greater than I am! He could easily have nudged mom to have her call 911. He could easily have arranged for someone to take her to the hospital for a Lasix IV. He could have taken over anytime during the swelling of my mom's legs.

It was prideful of me to think that only I had that control.

God had His own plans for mom's life and for mom's death. HE knew what was best for my mom. I had to trust that God did what HE KNEW was best, not what I thought was best.

I needed to become grateful instead of prideful. I needed to give God credit for always making right decisions.

"From the rising of the sun unto the going down of the same the Lord's name is to be praised." (Psalm 113:3)

"O give thanks unto the Lord…make known his deeds among the people.
Sing unto him…
Glory ye in his holy name: let the heart of them rejoice that seek the Lord.
Seek the Lord, and his strength…

Remember his marvelous works that he hath done…

…Praise ye the Lord." (Psalm 105:1-5,45)

November 5, the year mom died

God keeps reminding me that HE is in control of death. He is in control of the earth, including death.

> "That men may know that thou, whose name alone is JEHOVAH, art the most high over all the earth." (Psalm 83:18)
> "…thou, Lord, art most high for evermore."
> (Psalm 92:8)

February 5, about 2 years after mom's death

About two years into this grief, a friend of mine was facing grief similar to mine—grief mixed with self-blame, self-incrimination. We both felt that our loved ones would be alive if we had done things differently. Though 400 miles apart, we helped each other as we rediscovered and shared God's truths. My friend's Christian counselor had reminded her that God is in control. The pastor in Pennsylvania had reminded me that God is in control. Together my friend and I

helped each other assimilate God's truths—
to apply God's wise words to our lives.

Year after year of my grief, God taught me more and more. God's truths were reiterated to me over and over by many people. Gradually the truths sank into my brain and into my life.

I realized more and more what a good life mom had had. God gave her good health for many years.

Towards the end of her life, mom became almost blind with macular degeneration.

Recently I found a note reminding me to take mom to the ear doctor. She'd had to wear hearing aids and, even with them, she didn't hear well. That reminded me that she is seeing well in heaven and hearing well—she no longer needs hearing aids. She is now free of her fears. She will never be lonely.

July 5, four months after mom died

I realized she won't worry anymore. She will still be able to take walks. She will be able to enjoy eternal life. Maybe there are wintergreen berries, apricot jam, chocolate pie, and chocolate bars in heaven, especially "Milky Way" candy bars (one of her favorite candy bars) to eat while watching the stars of the real Milky Way of the sky.

"He that believeth on him is not condemned…" (John 3:18)

Jesus said, "Let not your heart be troubled: ye believe in God, believe also in me.

In my Father's house are many mansions…I go to prepare a place for you." (John 14:1-2)

"They shall hunger no more, neither thirst any more…" (Revelation 7:16)

"…and God himself shall be with them…

And God shall wipe away all tears from their eyes;" and there shall be no more death, neither sorrow, nor crying, neither shall there be any more pain: for the former things are past away.

…I will give unto him that is athirst of the fountain of the water of life freely." (Revelation 21:3-4,6)

Death is a certain event—people, pets, plants—everything has a lifespan that ends in death.

"To every thing there is a season…

A time to be born, and a time to die…" (Ecclesiastes 3:1-2)

"And as it is appointed unto men once to die, but after this the judgment…" (Hebrews 9:27)

> As David said, "But I trusted in thee, O Lord:
> I said, Thou art my God. My times are in thy
> hand…" (Psalm 31:14-15)

Back at the beginning of chapter 17, I wrote: "I never seem to be able to forget that last Friday I saw my mom alive. I will probably always regret my being in a hurry that day."

I did continue to frequently regret my actions—and lack of actions—that Friday before my mom died. Just think about how many minutes, hours, days, and weeks I wasted on regretting. I have made lots of progress in stopping my regretting about being in a hurry that Friday.

I wasted so much time on self-blame. I realize that by not allowing myself to grieve properly, I ended up in long-lasting discouragement, probably depression. If others blame us for causing a person's death, we can start believing the accusation and feeling we don't deserve to grieve. Self-abuse can have the same effect.

> January 10, ten months after my mother's death
> I wasted months of the time God gave me
> dwelling on guilt—both real and false. I
> believed she died because of my neglect, but
> the truth was that God is in control of death.

It was ten months before I started to realize
how much time I was wasting on regretting.

Lies can have a big influence on people—lies that we tell
ourselves and lies that others tell about us.

David had enemies who lied. He wrote about it in the
Bible, how he talked to God about it, prayed about it.

> "…O Lord…
> …deliver me from the hand of mine enemies,
> and from them that persecute me.
> Let the lying lips be put to silence; which speak
> grievous things proudly and contemptuously
> against the righteous." (Psalm 31:14-15,18)

Sometimes I was my worst enemy. Sometimes I lied to
myself about myself. Self-deceit can be just as injurious as the
lies of other people. I told myself over and over what a terrible
person I was.

I finally realized that by believing my lies, I was pleasing
the devil, who likes deceit, thrives on lies. Satan wanted me to
waste time dwelling on the past, so I wouldn't use the time to
serve God in the present.

> "…be vigilant; because your adversary the
> devil, as a roaring lion, walketh about,
> seeking whom he may devour…" (I Peter 5:8)

When doubts about myself arose, I began to compare them with God's truths to determine if what I was thinking was true or a lie. The Bible is a book of truths.

> "…it was impossible for God to lie…" (Hebrews 6:18)

> "…discern both good and evil." (Hebrews 5:14)

I kept deleting lies from my life.
I kept inserting God's truths into my life.

I kept blaming myself for mom's death. I wouldn't forgive myself for anything I did wrong or failed to do right. I kept blaming myself for wrongs I actually didn't do.

We could be on our own deathbed and still be wasting time on self-condemnation.

Paul in the Bible had been cruel to Christians, but, when he became a Christian, he didn't waste time dwelling on his past sins.

> Paul said, "…this one thing I do, **forgetting** those things which are behind, and reaching forth unto those things which are before, I **press toward** the mark for the prize of

the high calling of God in Christ Jesus."
(Philippians 3:13-14)

I thought of Lot's wife looking back as she and Lot left the cities that had been full of sin—Sodom and Gomorrah—that were burning. She died!

> "But his wife looked back from behind him, and she became a pillar of salt." (Genesis 19:26)

When we look back, it's as though we're living a "dead life." "Dead life" might seem like words with opposite meanings, but constantly remembering the past is like trying to live in the past.

I thought about the times when I've looked backwards while walking or riding a bike. I have fallen and gotten injured.

Dwelling on the past can result in hurting our Christian walk for God and tarnish our lives as ambassadors for Christ. "Now then we are ambassadors for Christ…" (II Corinthians 5:20) We are supposed to show the light of Christ in our lives, not dwell on the darkness of death. As Jesus said, "Ye are the light of the world…Let your light so shine before men, that they may see your good works, and glorify your Father which is in heaven." (Matthew 5:14,16) We shouldn't be like a flashlight with a dead battery.

God gives us the gift of each day that we live. We should live each day for Him.

Each day we need to live each minute to its fullest, not regretting the past or worrying about the future. We can't change the past or predict the future. We can concentrate on living for the Lord in the present.

> Yesterday is gone,
> Tomorrow's not here yet,
> So use today wisely.
>
> Thank You, God,
>   for today.
> Help me live it,
>   just Your way.

MAKE THE MOST OF EACH DAY—
LIVE IT GOD'S WAY.

I finally realized I had to put my regrets behind. I needed to file that page of my history and go forward for God.

Dying is a part of life, just as being born is a part of life—they are just on the opposite ends of the spectrum.

Death can help us appreciate each day that we live.

Satan wants us to waste time. God wants us to use time wisely.

"So teach us to number our days, that we may apply our hearts unto wisdom." (Psalm 90:12)

"Redeeming the time …" (Ephesians 5:16)

"As we have therefore opportunity, let us do good unto all men, especially unto them who are of the household of faith." (Galatians 6:10)

"…the night cometh, when no man can work." (John 9:4)

Thankfully, God has given me more time to live for Him, to serve Him, to work for Him.

Through this experience of coping with death, I gained more empathy for other mourners and this made me better able to encourage them. I go to funerals more often and hug the family members of the deceased person. I pray for them and sometimes tell them I am praying for them. Occasionally, I pray with them. Often I ask others to pray for them, too, and have them added to church prayer request lists. I sometimes send cards with a note, Scriptures, a song, a poem. Sometimes I make phone calls. Sometimes I visit. Sometimes I send a card or note to a stranger listed in an obituary as a survivor of the deceased person or mentioned in a newspaper article about a fatal accident or other tragedy. I learned to encourage others as I was encouraged, to comfort others as I was comforted.

> "…the God of all comfort;
> Who comforteth us in all our tribulation, that we may be able to comfort them which are in any trouble, by the comfort wherewith we ourselves are comforted of God." (II Corinthians 1:3-4)

January 10, almost a year after my mom died

> In a note sent to me to thank me for a sympathy card I sent to a lady when her mom died, the lady said her mom would be "sorely missed." Those words reminded me of the meaning of the word "sore." A death is like a sore that is hard to heal. Then a scab forms. A memory returns, and the scab is scuffed off, and the sore has to heal again.

Psalm 147:3 tells us how God heals our broken hearts. "He healeth the broken in heart, and bindeth up their wounds." (Here the word "wounds" refers to "griefs" in Hebrew.)

Going through a previous loss of a loved one, I wrote a song, "Jesus Guides Me." Recently I wrote a poem about a dove, a mourning dove. Both the song and the poem can be a comfort to mourners. Sometimes I send this song and poem to people who are mourning or people who are hurting in other ways. I plan to include the song in the appendix of this book. I hope the song can be scanned in.

The loss of my mom prepared me to write this book. Emotionally, this book was really difficult for me to write—I relived those difficult days. Even so, I'm thankful God was able to use me in this way.

> "And we know that all things work together for good to them that love God, to them who are the called according to his purpose." (Romans 8:28)

I still haven't gone to the cemetery.

Several times a friend has offered to go with me.

Visits to a grave help some people and are hard on others. Some people visit graves of loved ones and feel comforted; the effect is now the opposite on me.

We all handle grief in different ways and for different lengths of time.

However, I had to return to mom's house this summer, and I was finally ready—six years after her death.

For six years, Jim (my husband) patiently took care of mom's house—grass, snow, paint, repairs—lots of work for him. Jim had already done these tasks for my mom since my dad had died about twenty-five years earlier. It was a LOT of work for a LONG time.

Our oldest son wanted to buy the house and asked me to save it for him. I had saved it for him for six years, but, due to a series of hard situations, he was still not financially ready to take on a house loan.

For the last five of those years, we rented the house. Then the renters moved out. We could no longer keep up on all the expenses of the empty house—taxes, insurance, utilities, so Jim spent six months updating and restoring the interior of the house to sell it.

Thankfully, at last I was finally ready to return to the house—I had healed a lot from the grief. The kitchen walls and cupboards had been repainted by the renters and Jim had put new white linoleum in the kitchen. He'd put a new off-white rug in the living room. In some ways, the house no longer looked like mom's house. Mom had given the 1880s house an old-fashioned look with warm browns and golds. The renter chose the cool colors—aqua and white—a modern-looking décor.

Most of my mom's personal possessions had been boxed by a friend after the funeral. Some of mom's furniture was still in the house.

Our renters, who had moved to another state, had left quite a few of their belongings behind, especially craft supplies in the house and Christmas decorations in the big barn. It took a long time to go through their possessions, but, emotionally, it wasn't hard, because the items hadn't belonged to my mom.

Part of the barn contained my mom's belongings. The formerly neat boxes had since been re-stacked haphazardly by the renters with some of the contents strewn on the floor. Mom's furniture had been restacked many layers deep on top of the boxes.

Jim Sr. and Jim Jr. carefully took down the stacked the furniture. Then Jim Jr. and I went through the loose items on the floor. Jim Jr. wanted to keep all those items reminding him of his grandparents. As we worked together, Jimmy often told me what happy memory an item brought to him. He was so thrilled to find a little dog figurine and some miniature furniture he had made for his grandmother. Hearing about his many happy memories, my glad memories outnumbered the sad memories as I prepared the estate sale. He wanted to keep most of the boxed items, so that made it much easier for me emotionally, not having to go completely through many of the boxes. People think so differently. The possessions made our son happy and sometimes stirred up my old grief.

As it was, it took me many weeks to sort out the craft and Christmas items and tag lots of things for the estate sale, so that took my mind off the grief. We sold a few bigger items, such as beds, ahead of time to make more room to set up the sale.

Hundreds of people came to the two-day sale which we extended two days the following weekend. Jim and I handled the sale and all the pre-sale advertising. Because it was such a busy time, my mind was more on the sale and less on memories.

Other good things happened that same year—six years after mom died. Jim and I received three more grandchildren— all born within four months of each other, one grandchild every two months!

In March our youngest son and his wife had a girl, Rebecca.

Then in May, our oldest grandson and his wife had a baby girl, Jaimelynn.

As mentioned before, Sorya was born in April and Suthin in May.

Both of my parents were born in May and both died in March, so spring used to be a sad time for me.

Now it's great to look forward to the spring birthdays of Rebecca, Sorya, Suthin, and Jaimelynn.

Then in July, our oldest son had another son, Samuel, the month my maternal grandmother was born (the one with whom I grew up in our duplex house).

(Our oldest grandson, James III was born in October.)

What a blessing—three babies in one year—and born in months that usually brought sad memories. What a wonderful way to cancel out sad memories and replace them with glad memories.

I am healing in many ways. I'm even able to eat wintergreen berries without feeling guilty. As I wrote this, I just had another insight, maybe God, Who created wintergreen plants here on earth, also has wintergreen plants in heaven. I realized that if

God wanted mom to have wintergreen berries in heaven, He would provide them for her—anytime, not just in the spring and autumn when they are ripe at our camp. (Wintergreen berries ripen in the fall, but last all winter in the snow—the leaves stay green, too—and then the berries plump up bigger with the melted snow and spring rains.) "…God, who giveth us richly all things to enjoy…" (I Timothy 6:17)

God has never promised that life will be perfect. In the Bible Jesus states, "…In the world ye shall have tribulation: but be of good cheer; I have overcome the world." (John 16:33)

As obstacles in life keep coming, I need to keep remembering and applying what I have learned.

I need to remember God's timing is <u>always</u> right—God is never wrong.

I need to keep remembering that God loves me, even when I sin.

I need to remember that God forgives me when I confess my sins.

I need to keep on stopping to be angry with my self and keep on forgiving myself.

I need to always stop wasting time regretting, leave the past behind, and go forward for God.

God forms us before we are born, and our spirit returns to Him when we die.

"The great God that formed all things…" (Proverbs 26:10)

"…thou hast covered me in my mother's womb." (Psalm 139:13)

"…the spirit shall return unto God who gave it." (Ecclesiastes 12:7)

Mom was born in the spring and died in the spring. God planted her in the month of May and harvested her in the month of March. As Ecclesiastes 3:2 says, "…a time to plant, and a time to pluck up that which is planted…."

I got my mother when I was conceived and lost her when she died. As Ecclesiastes 3:6 says, "A time to get, and a time to lose…."

The book of Ecclesiastes has been a real comfort to me.

"To every thing there is a season…
A time to be born, and a time to die…
A time to weep, and a time to laugh;
a time to mourn, and a time to dance…"
Ecclesiastes 3:1-2,4

I'm not quite dancing yet, but, even as far back as December of the year mom died, I could say it was getting a bit easier every day.

When mom died, this is how I felt.

"Give ear to my prayer, O God…
My heart is sore pained within me: and
the terrors of death are fallen upon me.
Fearfulness and trembling are come upon me, and
horror hath overwhelmed me.
And I said, Oh that I had wings like a dove!
for then I would fly away, and be at rest.
Lo, then would I wander far off, and
remain in the wilderness. Selah.
I would hasten to my escape
from the windy storm and tempest."
Psalm 55:1,4-8

This is how I feel now.

"…O God…
"From the end of the earth will I cry unto thee,
when my heart is overwhelmed:
lead me to the rock that is higher than I.
For thou hast been a shelter for me, and
a strong tower from the enemy.
I will abide in thy tabernacle for ever:
I will trust in the covert of thy winds. Selah."
Psalm 61:2-4

God keeps His promises.

"Blessed are they that mourn:
for they shall be comforted."
Matthew 5:4
"…weeping may endure for a night,
but joy cometh in the morning."
Psalm 30:5

I don't have all the answers to coping with death and recovering from grief, but God does. God's words in the Bible are guaranteed to bring good results. **GOD'S WORD WORKS!**

We need to listen to God by reading His words in the Bible.

"So shall my word be that goeth forth out of my mouth:
it shall not return unto me void,
but it shall accomplish that which I please, and
it shall prosper in the thing whereto I sent it."
Isaiah 55:11

We need to talk to God. We need to trust God.

"Trust in him at all times;
ye people, pour out your heart before him:
God is a refuge for us. Selah."
Psalm 62:8

Seven years after my mom died, I was looking up Scriptures for the Bible study in the appendix of this book, and I got another insight (the more we read the Bible, the more insights we get). I was reading John, chapter 11.

Lazarus was the brother of Mary and Martha and a friend of Jesus. Lazarus got sick and died. Mary and Martha were probably with him when he died.

Jesus arrived when Lazarus had already been in the grave for four days. (verses 17, 20)

Martha said to Jesus, "…Lord, if thou hadst been here, my brother had not died." (verse 21)

Mary also said to Jesus, "…Lord, if thou hadst been here, my brother had not died." (verse 32)

Both sisters knew they couldn't save their brother's life, but they also knew Jesus could have saved their brother's life.

People do not have that power—not Mary or Martha (sisters of Lazarus), not Mary Goloversic, not anybody.

Jesus, the Son of God, even while living on earth, had the power to determine life or death.

Jesus, Himself, said, "…All power is given unto me in heaven and in earth."

(See John 11:22-44 for the rest of the story.)

A Note to You, the Reader

Each day the sad memories lessen and the good memories bring more happiness than sorrow.

With God's Words in the Bible and God's help and the help of all the people He brought into my life, I am healing.

Mary Goloversic

You, too, can heal—in God's way and in God's time.

With love and prayer,
Mary Goloversic

"The Lord bless thee, and keep thee:
The Lord make his face to shine upon thee, and
be gracious unto the:
The Lord lift up his countenance upon thee, and
give thee peace." (Numbers 6:24-26)

APPENDIX

"The Dove" (poem)

"Let Jesus Guide" (song lyrics)

Comforting Bible Verses for Grief

Some of God's Promises

Workshop to Cope with Death and Recover from Grief

Salvation and Success (pamphlet)

THE DOVE

by

Mary Goloversic

As soft as the gray feather of a dove,
Our Father's love floats down from above.
As gentle as the coo of a dove,
God's words in the Bible speak of His love.
God's actions and words show His love every day,
So let's all show we love Him in each our own way.

A dove symbolizes peace, and at peace we can be,
When we each pray to God—you and me.
God provides for the doves fresh water and food,
And provides for His people all that is good.
May we nest in the home He provides here on earth,
And then settle in heaven, a permanent berth.

A few years after my mom died, I saw a mourning dove near our home, and I wrote this poem. It was based on these Scriptures.

God said, "…I have loved thee with an everlasting love…" (Jeremiah 31:3)
"Be careful for nothing; but in every thing by prayer and supplication with thanksgiving let your requests be made known unto God.
And the peace of God, which passeth all

understanding, shall keep your hearts and minds through Christ Jesus." (Philippians 4:6-7) "Ever good gift and every perfect gift is from above, and cometh down from the Father…" (James 1:17)

LET JESUS GUIDE

(lyrics and music by Mary Goloversic)

1.   Jesus loves me, Jesus guides me,
He is my Morning Star,
Jesus loves me, Jesus guides me,
He never goes afar.
Though the dawn shall turn to dusk,
I still know how much I must,
Just let Jesus lead me, let Jesus guide me,
He will never let me go.

2.   Jesus loves me, Jesus guides me,
He is my Morning Star,
Jesus loves me, Jesus guides me,
He never goes afar.
When the road I take is rough,
When the task I face is tough,
I let Jesus love me, let Jesus guide me,
He will never let me go.

3.   Jesus loves me, Jesus guides me,
He is my Morning Star,
Jesus loves me, Jesus guides me,
He never goes afar.
Through the cold and ice and snow,
And the dangers and the foe,
I let Jesus lead me, let Jesus guide me,
He will never let me go.

4.	Jesus loves me, Jesus guides me,
	He is my Morning Star,
	Jesus loves me, Jesus guides me,
	He never goes afar.
	As down the valley I go,
	To what depth I do not know,
	I let Jesus lead me, let Jesus guide me,
	He will never let me go.

5.	Jesus loves me, Jesus guides me,
	He is my Morning Star,
	Jesus loves me, Jesus guides me,
	He never goes afar.
	As up the mountain I go,
	To His blessings I soon will know,
	I let Jesus lead me, let Jesus guide me,
	He will never let me go.

6.	I will love Him, I will love you,
	Just as I love myself.
	'Cause He tells me, in the Bible.
	That we must love enough.
	Though I might feel very low,
	And my progress seems so slow,
	With Jesus leading, with Jesus guiding,
	I will have success I know.

COMFORTING BIBLE
VERSES FOR GRIEF

"Give ear to my prayer, O God…

My heart is sore pained within me: and the terrors of death are fallen upon me.

Fearfulness and trembling are come upon me, and horror hath overwhelmed me.

And I said, Oh that I had wings like a dove! For then I would fly away, and be at rest.

Lo, then would I wander far off, and remain in the wilderness. Selah.

I would hasten to my escape from the windy storm and the tempest."

Psalm 55:1,4-8

"From the end of the earth will I cry unto thee, when my heart is overwhelmed: lead me to the rock that is higher than I.

For thou hast been a shelter for me, and a strong tower from my enemy.

I will abide in thy tabernacle for ever: I will trust in the covert of thy wings. Selah."

Psalm 61:2-4

"Praise the Lord…He healeth the broken in heart, and bindeth up their wounds." Psalm 147:1,3

"…weeping may endure for a night, but joy cometh in the morning." Psalm 30:5

"Blessed are they that mourn: for they shall be comforted." Matthew 5:4

SOME OF GOD'S PROMISES

"He that believeth on him is not condemned…" John 3:18

Jesus said, "Let not your heart be troubled: ye believe in God, believe also in me.

In my Father's house are many mansions…I go to prepare a place for you." John 14:1-2

"They shall hunger no more, neither thirst any more…" Revelation 7:16

"…and God himself shall be with them…

And God shall wipe away all tears from their eyes: and there shall be no more death, neither sorrow, nor crying, neither shall there be any more pain: for the former things are past away.

…I will give unto him that is athirst of the fountain of the water of life freely." Revelation 21:3-4,6

WORKSHOP TO COPE WITH DEATH AND RECOVER FROM GRIEF

Note:

The topic information in the "Workshop to Cope with Death and Recover from Grief" can be copied on note cards or paper to use at the workshop and as as daily memos.

Note:

This same information can also be used alone, with a friend, or any small group.

The leader opens with a welcome and prayer.

> Thank you for coming. We will start the meeting with prayer.
>
>> Dear God, Thank You for bringing each of us together today as we grieve the passing of a loved one. Help us to recognize the lies in our grief and understand how to apply Your words to our lives. In Jesus' Name, amen.

Everyone reads the information in Topic 1.

Then the leader asks question 1 about the topic and allows time for discussion. This continues for the rest of the questions. Then everyone goes on to Topic 2.

Repeat this until all 9 topics are done.

We will close in prayer.

> Dear God, Thank You for caring about us to much that You gave us Scriptures to comfort us in our grief and to guide us as we grieve. In Jesus' Name, amen.

Question 1 about my past failure:

What did I ever think or say or do that the lie/lies say?

Question 2 about my past success:

What did I ever think or say or do that the truth/truths say?

Question 3 about my present success:

How did I make progress to success recently by applying God's truth?

Question 4 about my plans for more success:

What do I plan to think or say or do now to carry out the truth?

Topic 1

Lie: Grief will last forever.

Truth: Intense grief will pass.

Psalm 30:5 "…weeping may endure for a night, but joy cometh in the morning."

Ecclesiastes 3:1,4 "To every thing there is a season…a time to mourn, and a time to dance…"

Topic 2

Lie: I don't have anyone to comfort me.

Truth: God's words in the Bible will comfort you and perhaps God will send people into your life to comfort you.

Matthew 5:4 "Blessed are they that mourn: for they shall be comforted."

Topic 3

Lie: I can't get through this grief.

Truth: With God's help, you can overcome your grief.

Philipppians 4:13 "I can do all things through Christ which strengtheneth me."

Topic 4

Lie: I will be guilty forever because I sinned—I hurt and/or neglected someone who died.

Truth: God forgives, and because God, Who is wise, can forgive me, I can forgive myself.

I John 1:9 "If we confess our sins, he is faithful and just to forgive us our sins, and to cleanse us from all unrighteousness."

Topic 5

Lie: I should be punished because I am so terrible—I hurt and/or neglected the person who died.

Truth: God is the judge of people.

Psalm 50:6 "…God is the judge himself…"

Topic 6

Lie: I can never forgive someone who hurt and/or neglected the deceased person.

Truth: God commands us to forgive, and He doesn't ask us to do anything we cannot do; God forgives us and others and we should follow His example and forgive.

Ephesians 4:32 "And be ye kind one to another, tenderhearted, forgiving one another, even as God for Christ's sake hath forgiven you."

Topic 7

Lie: I stay angry at the person who committed suicide.

Truth: Forgive.

Ephesians 4:32 "...forgiving one another, even as God for Christ's sake hath forgiven you."

Topic 8

Lie: Other people who hurt and/or neglected the person who died should be punished; maybe I should punish the people myself.

Truth: God is the judge of people and He tells us to obey authorities, such at the judges in courts who determine whether or not to punish and what the punishment should be.

Psalm 50:6 "...God is the judge himself..."

Hebrews 13:17 "Obey them that have the rule over you..."

Topic 9

Lie: We have the power to control life and death, even what day a person will die.

Truth: God controls everything—even the day of birth and the day of death.

Acts 1:7 "...It is not for you to know the times or the seasons, which the Father hath put in his own power."

SUCCESS AND SALVATION PAMPHLET

success= being the person God wants you to be, not what you or others want you to be.

8 Steps for Success

1. **Read truths in Bible**
   "Search the Scriptures…" John 5:39
2. **Recognize lies**
   "Let no man deceive you…" II Thessalonians 2:3
3. **Repent**
   "…I will be sorry for my sin." Psalm 38:18
4. **Replace**
   "…put off…the old man…put on…the new man…" Ephesians 4:22,24
5. **Love**
   "…love one another…" John 15:12
6. **Forgive**
   "…forgiving one another…" Ephesians 4:32
7. **Communicate**
   "…speaking the truth in love…" Ephesians 4:15
8. **Help**
   "…come and help…" Luke 5:7

Jesus is needed to be successful. You need Jesus. Believe this Bible verse:

> "For God so loved the world, that he gave his only begotten Son, that whosoever believeth in him should not perish, but have everlasting life." John 3:16

Pray a prayer like this:

> Dear God, I sin. I am sorry I sinned. I believe Jesus died on the cross to pay for my sins and He rose again. I accept Jesus as my Savior. Thank you."

Printed in the United States
By Bookmasters